THE SULTAN'S KITCHEN
A Turkish Cookbook

BY

Özcan Ozan

~~~~~~~~~~~~~~~~

Photographs by Carl Tremblay

PERIPLUS

EDITIONS

~~~~~~~~~~~~~~~

I dedicate this book to my wife Faith Ozan
for all her patience, support, and encouragement;
to my sons, Evren and Aydın Ozan, and to
my mother Müşerref Ozan.

First published in 1998 by Periplus Editions (HK) Ltd., with editorial offices at 153 Milk Street, Boston, Massachusetts 02109.

Library of Congress Cataloging-in-Publication Data

Ozan, Özcan.
    The sultan's kitchen : a Turkish cookbook / by Özcan Ozan ;
photographs by Carl Tremblay. — 1st ed.
        p.   cm.
    Includes index.
    ISBN 962-593-223-2 (hardcover)
    1. Cookery, Turkish.   2. Sultan's Kitchen (Restaurant : Boston,
Mass.) I. Title.
TX725.T8092 1998
641.59561—dc21

97-52132
CIP

Publisher: Eric Oey

Creative Director: Christina Ong

Project Editor: Isabelle Bleecker

Project Assistant: Deane Norton

Book Designer: Jill Winitzer

Food Stylist: George Simons

Production: Kim Grogan, Mary Chia

Backgrounds by Associated Quirks, Boston

Distributed by

USA	Japan	Southeast Asia
Charles E. Tuttle Co., Inc.	Tuttle Shokai Ltd.	Berkeley Books Pte. Ltd.
RR 1 Box 231-5	1-21-13, Seki	5 Little Road #08-01
North Clarendon, VT 05759	Tama-ku, Kawasaki-shi	Singapore 536983
Tel.: (802) 773-8930	Kanagawa-ken 214, Japan	Tel.: (65) 280-3320
Fax.: (802) 773-6993	Tel.: (044) 833-0225	Fax.: (65) 280-6290
	Fax.: (044) 822-0413	

First Edition
1 2 3 4 5 6 7 8 9 10   98 99 00 01 02 03 04 05 06 07

Printed in Singapore

CONTENTS

~~~~~~~~~~~~~~~~~~~~~~~~

PREFACE

~~~~~~~~~~~~~~~~~~~~~~~~~~~~~~~

AS A CHILD GROWING UP ON THE AEGEAN SEA, I was naturally more interested in the business of childhood than in appreciating my surroundings. Now, however, reflecting back as an adult living in another country, I am very appreciative of the myriad Aegean influences that shaped my early years and especially thankful for ones that fostered my passion for good food.

İzmir, the city where I was born and raised, is ancient Smyrna. Greek and Roman ruins that are mostly taken for granted by the residents are dotted throughout the city. Similarly, the grandeur of the Ottoman Empire left its mark on the city's art and architecture, on the lifestyle of its people, and on its cuisine.

Turkish cuisine ranks as one of the three great world cuisines (along with French and Chinese) and has a long and complex history. The result has been the development of a varied array of dishes with flavors that are both familiar and surprising to the Western palate. Despite its ancient roots, the Turkish diet is a very healthy one, even by today's standards, with its emphasis on eating a variety of foods and using fresh ingredients.

The typical Aegean arrangement of daily shopping at small specialty groceries and shops creates a lot of noisy, colorful, and aromatic hustle and bustle that is the fabric of day-to-day life. Sharing evening meals is at the core of Turkish family life. Countless seaside and outdoor cafés and restaurants provide backdrops for the enjoyment of food, drink, and conversation. So, as I look back with some nostalgia, I think that the natural beauty of the region, the classical and Ottoman aesthetics, the panoramic presence of food, and food's critical role in family and society have all contributed to my becoming a chef by profession.

As is true for many professional chefs, my first teacher was my mother. I was raised modestly and traditionally, and we lived simply on my father's wages and my mother's domesticity. Having come to İzmir from a nearby village, my mother brought rural, traditional recipes to the city along with her incomparable standards for freshness and variety and respect for food. She often took me with her on shopping expeditions (sometimes lasting for hours) as she inspected and chose vegetables, fruits, cheeses, olives, grains, edible wild greens, herbs, spices, poultry, and fish. Returning home, my mother would get to work in the kitchen, spending long hours preparing family meals of stuffed vegetables cooked with olive oil, böreks (savory pastries), vegetable stews cooked with meat, hearty soups, pilafs, many different eggplant dishes (especially in summer), and puddings. Eventually, I was sent alone to do some shopping (flattered that she would trust my selections!), and my interest in cooking grew into summer jobs at resort hotels on the Aegean. I recall my teenage fascination with the inner workings of those large kitchens, taking great pleasure in the many facets of food preparation and the staff camaraderie.

Later I went to Europe and cooked for six years, then returned to İzmir and cooked for another four. When I arrived in Boston in the early 1980s, the city was becoming receptive to international cuisines, and health consciousness was becoming a major restaurant consideration. I acquired space in Boston's Financial District and opened Sultan's Kitchen, specializing in Turkish cuisine. Sultan's Kitchen was not only the first Turkish restaurant in Boston; it was also one of the first open-kitchen restaurants in the city, in keeping with typical Aegean restaurant design.

Sultan's Kitchen has been in operation for sixteen years, and my goals have not wavered over time. I enjoy introducing Turkish cuisine to new customers, exposing them to bits of Turkish culture through music and decor, and, most important, preserving the high standards and authenticity of Turkish cuisine that I experienced as a child. The recipes presented in this book have all appeared on my restaurant's menu at one time or another. I am always varying the menu according to what is plentiful in the market, but what I hope never varies is the quality and presentation I have worked to preserve and share in Boston.

By way of this cookbook, I invite people who have never tasted Turkish food to enjoy this unique and delicious cuisine. And I hope it will make you agree with me that eating is, after all, one of life's greatest pleasures.

INTRODUCTION

~~~~~~~~~~~~~~~~~~~~~~~~~~~~~~~

IT ALMOST GOES WITHOUT SAYING THAT WHEN you eat in Turkey, you eat well. Good food is an important part of Turkish culture, and if you walk the streets of any city, you will see and smell it all around you. Tea shops and outdoor cafés abound. Colorful streetside displays of produce, small specialty food shops, neighborhood bakeries, street vendors, and daily shoppers are typical throughout the country.

Partly in Europe and partly in Asia, Turkey stands at the crossroads of many cultures. Istanbul is at the southeastern end of Europe, and Ankara, the capital, is located in Anatolia, which comprises the peninsula of Asia Minor. Turkey has a long coastline along the Mediterranean Sea in the south, the Black Sea in the north, and the Aegean Sea in the west. High mountain ranges run parallel to the sea in the south and in the north. The eastern part is very mountainous, and there is a vast plateau in the center of the country, which comprises Anatolia. To the north, it is surrrounded by Russia and the Russian republics, in the east Iran, in the south Syria, Lebanon, Iraq, and Israel, in the west, Greece and Bulgaria.

Turkey is a land of many civilizations that have come and gone, leaving behind the ruins of ancient cities. The Turks originally migrated from central Asia and settled in Asia Minor, where they were influenced by the presence of other cultures, among them the Hittites, Byzantines, Greeks, Romans, Selçuks, and Ottomans.

In 1453, relatively recently in terms of Turkish history, the Ottoman tribe conquered Constantinople (now Istanbul) and the Ottoman Empire ruled much of the medieval world. At the Topkapı Palace in Constantinople, great chefs refined the dishes that constitute today's Turkish cuisine. During this time, the culinary arts were an important part of the daily life in the sultan's courts. With the infinite variety of fish, fowl, meat, fruit, grains, and vegetables that were available in Turkey, Ottoman chefs competed to create innovative new dishes for the sultans.

The Ottoman Empire reached its height of power during the reign of Sultan Süleyman the Magnificent, who added a kitchen with six domes to the Topkapı Palace and employed more than a thousand cooks. It was natural for the court kitchen to be influenced by Western culture, and the Europeans were also influenced by the Ottomans. In fact, open-air cafés are an example of an Ottoman tradition brought to Europe. These culinary legacies created a rich cuisine that was admired and carried into the Middle East, the Balkans, parts of Russia and Europe, and North Africa.

Turkish food is wonderfully spiced and has complex flavors. Turks are used to eating well, and their standards are high. There are some sophisticated recipes that require skill and time, but most can be prepared easily. There are unusual flavor combinations—eggplant with garlic and yogurt, for example—and beautiful presentation is an important consideration. The Turkish diet, in which a great variety of foods and more vegetables, fruit, beans, and grains than meat are eaten, is a very healthy one. The cuisine's most important characteristic is its reliance on very fresh ingredients, and the cooking methods bring out the natural flavors of those ingredients. Vegetables and fruit are eaten during the season in which they are grown and are purchased daily. Fish is eaten on the day it is caught.

Lamb, fish, and beans are sources of protein, and bread is a staple. Garlic, onions, spices, and fresh and dried herbs are used as seasonings. Yogurt is eaten in sauces and drinks, and cheeses, especially sheep's milk cheeses and soft white cheese (like the Greek feta) are also a regular part of meals. Different foods are served in different seasons: summer dishes use fresh produce, are lighter, and are served chilled or at room temperature while winter dishes are heartier and heavier, using root vegetables and stewed beans and meats.

Eating habits vary from region to region, but a typical day in Turkey often starts with a breakfast of freshly baked bread, sliced tomatoes, several types of olives, cheese, and jams. There may be soft-boiled eggs, or *böreks,* the stuffed savory pastries that are also eaten throughout the day. Breakfast is served with Turkish tea.

Lunch and dinner may both start with a soup, which is so popular that there are many specialized soup shops, called *corbaçı.* At dinner, soup maybe followed by a main course of grilled meat, chicken, or fish, and served with pilaf and salad. Dessert is typically fruit compote (stewed, dried fruits like raisins or apricots), fresh fruit, or pudding.

For special occasions or parties, tables are spread with *meze,* a selection of appetizers that consists of seasonal vegetables cooked with olive oil, pureed or stuffed vegetables, seafood, or böreks. Baklava and other sweet desserts are most often served on special occasions.

In the past bread was used instead of forks to eat meals that were served on the floor, with the family sharing from a large tray. Today's eating customs are modern, but bread—pita, sourdough, and flat breads, to name a few—is still an important part of every meal. The best breads are found outside of the cities, in the small villages, because in urban areas traditional bread-making has given way to mass production.

During the day, snacks of böreks purchased at shops called *börekçi* are eaten with *ayran,* a tangy yogurt drink. Turkish tea is served throughout the day.

Each region of Turkey has its own cooking style and specialties. In eastern Turkey and Anatolia, the food is robust and spicy—not spicy like the flavor of hot peppers, but pungent and complex. In many parts of the region they use clarified butter, butter, and animal fat for cooking, especially the fat rendered from sheeps' tails. In this region, dishes are prepared with unusual seasonings like molasses, unripened grape juice, dried fruits, and loquats. Beans and yogurt are also used in much of the cuisine. Tandır Kebabı or Kuyu Kebabı, a specialty of Anatolia, is prepared by slowly grilling a young lamb in a tightly covered dirt pit. Anatolian cuisine is becoming more popular in other parts of Turkey.

In the Western and Mediterranean parts of Turkey, dishes are prepared with olive oil and include small amounts of meat that are always cooked with vegetables. Olive oil is the main ingredient and vegetables cooked in olive oil are popular. Chief among these are *dolmalar* (dolmas) and *sarmalar* (sarmas), which are stuffed or rolled leafy vegetables cooked with rice, black currants, pine nuts, herbs, and olive oil.

The Aegean and Mediterranean regions produce much of Turkey's fruit and the city of İzmir is known for its figs, grapes, fragrant Manisa *kırkağaç* melons, and large, sweet Bursa peaches. Fresh fruits are eaten before, after, and in between meals, and they are also made into compotes or jams, or are dried. I remember picking figs with my mother as a child. We would dry them and in the winter we would stuff each fig with a walnut and eat them for dessert.

~Mounds of fresh eggplants and string beans for sale

Olive trees are everywhere in the Aegean and Mediterranean regions of Turkey. They produce all types of olives: black, green, light reddish green, beige, and pink, which are served at all meals, and they are often garnished with a drizzle of oil, a squeeze of lemon juice, and a sprinkling of dried herbs.

Fish are plentiful in these coastal regions and it is prepared in many ways. Almost everybody has a charcoal grill at home, even in the high-rise apartment buildings where they are kept and used on balconies. (I recently saw a true example of the the old encountering the new when visiting my brother-in-law in İzmir, who was using a hair dryer to intensify the charcoal fire on his apartment balcony. He grilled *çipura,* a fish for which İzmir is famed. It was delicious!)

The flavors of Turkey have as broad a range as its many peoples and cultural influences. Some of these recipes are centuries old, and they have all evolved somewhat with time and with changing cooking methods. Despite the passage of time, these dishes are almost unmatched in their wholesomeness and rich flavors. The recipes I've collected here represent a sampling of Turkish cuisine. I am happy to share them with you, and welcome you to the world of Turkish food.

SUGGESTED MENUS

ALL MENUS SERVE 4–6 PEOPLE

~~~~~~~~~~~~~~~~~~~~~~~~~~~~~~~~

Summer dinner menu

SOUP: High Plateau Soup (page 60)

APPETIZER: Stuffed Eggplant (page 19)

MAIN COURSE: Char-Grilled Swordfish Shish Kebab (page 110) and White Rice Pilaf (page 115)

SALAD: Shepherd's Salad (page 127)

DESSERT: Pistachio Semolina Cake (page 139) and Turkish Coffee (page 150)

Winter dinner menu

SOUP: Red Lentil, Bulgur, and Mint Soup (page 66)

APPETIZER: Jerusalem Artichokes Cooked in Olive Oil (page 24)

MAIN COURSE: Pasha's Kofta (page 76) and Bulgur Pilaf with Peppers and Tomatoes (page 120)

SALAD: Daikon Radish Salad (128)

DESSERT: Baklava (page 137) and Turkish Coffee (page 150)

Summer lunch menu

Serve a sour cherry drink (page 151) or *ayran*, a yogurt drink (page 151), with this menu.

APPETIZER: Fried Eggplant and Green Peppers with Yogurt-Garlic and Tomato Sauces (page 20)

MAIN COURSE: Spicy Char-Grilled Kofta Shish Kebab (page 77) and Rice Pilaf with Chickpeas (page 115) and Onion Relish (page 15)

SALAD: Dandelion Salad (page 124)

DESSERT: Almond Pudding (page147)

Winter lunch menu

APPETIZER: Spicy Pureed Tomatoes (page 19)

MAIN COURSE: Lamb with White Beans in a Clay Pot (page 81) and White Rice Pilaf (page 115)

SALAD: Celeriac Salad (page 126)

DESSERT: Shredded Filo Dough with Walnuts (page 140)

DRINK: Turkish Tea (page 150)

~Previous page: A summer luncheon (see menu above) served with Raisin Compote (page 150) and Rustic Turkish Bread (page 46)

TURKISH INGREDIENTS

MOST OF THE INGREDIENTS USED IN TURKISH cuisine are not that unusual, and you will be able to find them in a well-stocked supermarket or gourmet shop. But there are a few items that you will need to buy in specialty or Middle Eastern food stores. See the list on page 153 for mail-order sources.

BEANS AND PEAS: Beans and peas are used widely in Turkish cooking, both fresh and dried. Some of the beans used in Turkey are slightly different, but I've given readily available alternatives in each recipe.

Dried beans and peas need to be soaked overnight to reduce their cooking time. Wash the beans and remove any pebbles or dirt. Place them in a pot or bowl with enough cold water so that the water level is 2 inches above the top of the beans. They can soak at room temperature, but refrigerate them if the weather is very warm. Leave them to soak overnight (8–10 hours), and discard anything that floats to the surface. The next day, drain the beans and wash them again.

If you don't have time to soak the legumes overnight, you can prepare them using the quick method: place 2 cups of beans with 6 cups of water in a large pot and boil for 2 minutes. Remove the pot from the heat and let the beans sit for 1 hour before cooking. See also Fava Beans.

BLACK CARAWAY SEEDS (ÇÖREK OTU): These small black seeds are also called black cumin or nigella seeds. They have an intense fragrance and flavor unlike that of any other spice. In Turkey, they are sprinkled on pita bread, rolls, and other breads before baking.

BULGUR (CRACKED WHEAT): This cracked wheat comes in fine, medium and coarse grinds. Sold in supermarkets either in bulk or in boxes, it is used for making various pilafs and is added to salads. Use the fine grind for making salads, and medium to coarse grinds for pilafs.

CLARIFIED BUTTER (SÜZME YAĞ): You can substitute regular butter wherever I have listed clarified butter in the ingredients lists, except in the desserts. I prefer to use clarified butter whenever melted butter is called for, especially in making pastries. Clarified butter lacks the impurities that cause butter to burn easily and turn black. Turkish desserts, such as baklava, keep longer at room temperature when they are made with clarified butter because the milk solids, which sour easily, have been removed.

To make 1 1/2 cups of clarified butter, melt a pound of butter in a saucepan over low heat until a white foam appears on the surface. Skim and discard the foam. Slowly pour the clarified butter in a bowl, leaving behind and discarding the milk solids that have collected at the bottom of the pan. It will keep for a few weeks stored in a cool place.

FRESH CORIANDER (KİŞNİŞ): This herb, which is sold in markets in this country under the Spanish name *cilantro*, is widely used in cooking in the southern and eastern parts of Turkey. Kişniş looks a bit like Italian flat-leafed parsley, but the leaves are more delicate. In Turkish cuisine, it lends its distinctive flavor to pilafs, salads, and soups. To keep it fresh for up to a week, place the coriander stems in a jar of water, cover with a plastic bag, and refrigerate.

EGGPLANT (PATLICAN): Eggplant has a special place in Turkish cuisine, and it is featured in a wide range of dishes. In Turkey, the eggplants are small, long, and thin and range in color from purple to almost black. These are stuffed or added to stews and pilafs. In these recipes, I've recommended using Italian eggplants, which are similar. Globe eggplants, called *bostan patlıcan*, are also used in Turkey, in recipes that call for the flesh to be pureed like in *beğendi*, a creamed eggplant accompaniment to meat.

I use eggplants imported from Holland because I find them fresher and less bitter than those grown here. When buying eggplants, make sure the skins are tight and smooth, without any dark spots. The stems should be green and fresh.

~ *Top row:* saffron, pistachio nuts, mastic, almonds
Second Row: pine nuts, *baharat*, black caraway seeds, vanilla crystals
Third Row: whole and ground sumac, dried mint, Turkish red pepper (from Maraş), red lentils
Fourth Row: ground cumin, Turkish red pepper (from Gaziantep), whole anise seeds

Because eggplants can have a bitter taste, it is a good idea to soak them before using them. This will also keep fried eggplant from absorbing too much oil. Place sliced eggplant in a bowl. Generously salt the slices, cover with cold water, and set aside for 30 minutes. Rinse the slices under cold running water, gently squeeze out the excess water, and pat them dry with paper towels.

FAVA BEANS (TAZE BAKLA): In summer, fresh young fava beans are cooked and simmered in olive oil and served with yogurt or Yogurt-Garlic Sauce (page 13). Older beans are shelled and cooked fresh. Dried fava beans are available year-round and come in two varieties: the large brown kind and the small light green or white ones, both of which need to be soaked before cooking. Fresh fava beans may be slightly difficult to obtain—they are also called *broad beans* and are usually available in the summertime, especially in Italian markets.

FETA CHEESE (BEYAZ PEYNIR): A semifirm cheese that crumbles easily, Turkish white cheese (the Greek version is feta cheese), is made from sheep's or goat's milk and then soaked in a brine mixture. Some white cheeses are softer or creamier than others, and the degree of saltiness can also vary considerably.

Before cooking with feta cheese, first rid it of some of its saltiness. Cut the cheese into chunks and soak it in warm water for about 20 minutes, changing the water several times. The best *beyaz peynir* in Turkey comes from northwestern Edirne.

FILO DOUGH (YUFKA): This is the dough that is used in many classic Turkish pastries, including baklava. It is made of flour, eggs, and water, and is rolled out as thin as paper. To get homemade filo (see page 136) to its characteristic thinness, it is rolled out first with a large thick rolling pin called a *merdane* and then a very thin rolling pin called an *oklava*. In Turkey, filo dough comes in various thicknesses, with the thicker doughs used for böreks.

Filo dough can be bought fresh in Middle Eastern supermarkets and frozen in most other supermarkets. Each package contains twenty to twenty-two sheets of dough. Thick filo dough, called *yufka,* is available by mail order.

To use frozen filo dough, let it stand in the box at room temperature for about 6 hours, or let it thaw in the refrigerator overnight. Remove the dough from the package and thaw for another hour without unrolling it. Because filo is so thin, it dries out easily. Therefore, keep the dough covered with a damp cloth.

SHREDDED FILO DOUGH (KADAYIF OR KADAIFI): *Kadayıf* dough is made with flour, milk, and water. The batter is poured through a fine sieve onto a large, moving hot steel plate, thereby creating its characteristic long strings and slightly cooked texture. It is available either fresh or frozen.

To use frozen kadayıf dough, let it stand in the box at room temperature for about 6 hours; then remove it from the box and let it thaw for another hour. Alternatively, let it thaw in the refrigerator overnight, remove from the box, and thaw for another hour. Divide the shredded filo dough in half by holding it upright and pulling it apart. Place the dough on a dry surface and cover it with a damp cloth to prevent it from drying out.

FISH: It is important to use fresh fish for the best flavor. When buying whole fish, the eyes should be bright and clear, not clouded, and the gills should be bright red and open. Make sure the skin is shiny and the flesh is firm.

When buying fillets, check that the flesh is firm, not spongy. They should not have any ammonia smell. Swordfish steaks should be white to light pinkish and firm.

GRAPE LEAVES (ASMA YAPRAĞI SALAMURASI): In Turkey, home cooks pick fresh grape leaves, which grow in the Aegean and Mediterranean regions of the country. After cleaning them, they blanch the leaves in water salted with sea salt. The leaves are then packed in a brine solution, in which they keep for as long as six months. Grape leaves are sold in most big supermarkets. Look for one-pound jars containing about eighty leaves. Opened jars keep for as long as a year, stored in the refrigerator.

Before cooking them, unroll the grape leaves and boil them for 1 minute to help remove some of the brine.

KASSERI CHEESE (KAŞAR PEYNİRİ): A semifirm cheese made from sheep's milk, kasseri is light yellow, very smooth, and elegant. It ranges from mild to sharp, in the same way that cheddar cheese does. In fact, a sharp cheddar makes an acceptable alternative. The best kasseri comes from the eastern Turkish town of Kars and the northwestern town of Edirne.

LAMB: Lamb is the most popular meat in Turkey, and it is consumed in greater quantities than chicken or beef. The best lamb is always the youngest you can get. When it is nine months to a year old, lamb is sold as mutton, and the flesh will be redder. Good lamb should have lightly rosy flesh and pure white fat around the edges. When buying it, look for smaller roasts—under six pounds with the bone in is best. (Lamb is tastier when it is cooked with the bone in.) Lamb from Australia and New Zealand is smaller and comes from younger animals than that sold in the United States.

MASTIC (SAKIZ): Mastic is a pale white resin from a small evergreen tree. People often chew it like chewing gum. It has a subtle flavor reminiscent of pine and is used to flavor puddings and ice creams. It is sold in small quantities in Middle Eastern supermarkets.

MINT LEAVES, DRIED (KURU NANE): Another important ingredient in Turkish cooking, dried mint is used far more widely than fresh mint. The dried ground mint sold in supermarkets lacks the fragrance and subtlety of the slightly crumbled imported leaves sold loose or in containers from Middle Eastern supermarkets.

OLIVE OIL: Olive oil is another of the staple ingredients in Turkish cuisine, and the four grades are used for different purposes. Olive oils vary in flavor, color, and aroma, depending on where the olives are grown, how the oil is processed, and the level of acidity.

Olives are delicate, and ideally they are hand-picked or are shaken from the trees and collected in nets spread underneath. The olives should be pressed within three days of harvesting because they grow more acidic if they sit too long. Traditionally the olives were crushed using huge round stones, but now it is done with mechanical presses.

Extra-virgin olive oil, the result of the first cold pressing of the olives, is the most expensive grade of oil and has an acidity of 0–1 percent. It ranges in color from emerald green to olive, and its flavor is fruity. I use it for seasoning, marinades, dressings, and drizzled over salads and cooked food just before serving.

Virgin olive oil is also from the first cold pressing of the olives, and is semifruity with a more pronounced olive flavor. It is lighter green than extra-virgin, with acidity between 2 and 3 percent, and is a bit less expensive. I use virgin olive oil for cooking.

Olive oil is a blend of refined olive oil from the second press of the olives and virgin olive oil. It is yellow and has less flavor. You can use this oil in sauces, delicately seasoned soups, and for subtly flavored dishes.

Olive pomace oil, or light olive oil, is the lowest and least expensive grade of olive oil. It is light yellow and has only a little flavor. Pomace is what remains of the olives after the second press. The pomace oil is extracted using solvents and is then blended with virgin olive oil. I use this oil for frying and sautéing.

PINE NUTS OR PIGNOLI (BEYAZ FISTIK): These small pale yellow nuts taste best when they are lightly browned in butter or olive oil (depending on the recipe). The best pine nuts have an elongated, even shape and uniform color. They are used in pilafs, stuffings, stuffed vegetables (*sarmalar* and *dolmalar),* and desserts.

ROSE WATER (GÜL SUYU): Distilled from fragrant rose petals, rose water is used in Turkish cooking to flavor milk puddings, drinks, and syrups. It can be purchased by the bottle in specialty shops. Look for pure rose water and be sure it is meant for culinary use rather than cosmetic use.

SEMOLINA (İRMİK): Made from durum wheat and sold in small boxes in supermarkets or in bulk in specialty stores, semolina comes in fine and coarse grinds.

SUMAC (SUMAK): These dried, crushed red berries give a slightly lemony and sour flavor to dishes. Sumac is also often used as a table condiment and sprinkled over grilled meats, chicken, and salads. Turkish sumac is unrelated to the poisonous shrub.

SÜZME YOGURT: Called *torba yoğurdu* in Turkish, this yogurt has been left to drain so that it becomes thick and creamy. It is used to make herb-flavored spreads, and it is also used in cooking.

To make 2 cups of thick yogurt, take 6 cups plain yogurt, line a large sieve with a double layer of cheesecloth, place the sieve over a large bowl, pour the yogurt into the sieve, and let it drip. In 1 hour the yogurt will start to get thick. Let the yogurt drain, covered and refrigerated, in the sieve overnight to get a very thick consistency.

TAHINI: Made from ground sesame seeds, tahini comes in both light and dark varieties, the latter being made from roasted ground sesame seeds. In Turkish cooking, light tahini is used in making hummus. It comes in jars or cans and is sold in regular supermarkets, health food stores, and Middle Eastern supermarkets.

TOMATO: Always buy tomatoes that are firm and have bright red skin. Some recipes call for skinned and seeded tomatoes. I remove the skin by peeling them with a sharp paring knife. To skin a large quantity of tomatoes quickly, plunge them in boiling water for about 30 seconds, take them out with a slotted spoon and put them into ice water for 20 seconds. Take them out of the ice water and with a sharp paring knife, score the skin once near the top of the tomato—the skin will split. Peel off the skin of each tomato in strips and remove the stem by cutting in a cone shape around it. Pat the tomatoes dry, and if you are planning to use them in a cold dish, refrigerate them. To remove the seeds, cut the tomatoes in quarters and use your fingertips to scrape them out.

TURKISH RED PEPPER, DRIED (KIRMIZI ACI BIBER): This ground or flaked red pepper is another seasoning, like garlic and onion, that has a special place in Turkish cuisine and is used in every kind of dish. It is slightly moist with a coarse texture and imparts aroma, heat, subtle pepper flavor, and a reddish color to dishes. Its flavor ranges from very hot, semihot, to mild and sweet, and it can be light red, dark red, purplish, and even black.

The best red peppers grow in southeastern Turkey near the cities of Maraş, Gaziantep, and Urfa, and the peppers of each area have a distinctive flavor and color. Urfa red peppers are roasted, and the pepper is black. In Maraş, the red peppers are crushed and rubbed with oil to impart flavor. The pepper is very aromatic and dark red. In Gaziantep the peppers are milder and lighter red.

The southeast of Turkey is known for its spicy dishes, and in other regions cooks simply use less pepper to produce milder variations. Don't be afraid to use Turkish red pepper because it's more flavorful than hot—more like the heat imparted by a good ground red pepper, which makes an acceptable substitute.

VANILLA CRYSTALS: Customarily used in Turkish cooking, this fine white powder has a stronger flavor and none of the alcohol found in vanilla extract. If you can't obtain it, use double the amount of vanilla extract instead.

~Turkish red pepper

SAUCES AND CONDIMENTS

~~~~~~~~~~~~~~~~

Sauces in Turkish cooking tend to be very simple and very fresh. Rarely is a sauce simmered for any length of time. Indeed, to preserve the freshness of tomatoes and herbs, sauces are usually made quickly just before a dish is served.

Ground pine nuts, garlic, olive oil, and lemon are combined to make Beyaz Fıstıklı Tarator (page 13), a delicious cold sauce that accompanies grilled fish and seafood. Terbiye (page 15), an egg and lemon sauce with a creamy, velvety texture and tangy flavor, is served with stuffed vegetables and stuffed grape leaves. Plain yogurt or yogurt flavored with raw garlic, Sarmısaklı Yoğurt Sos (page 13), is served as a simple sauce for grilled meats and vegetables, pilafs, savory pastries, and as a topping for cooked Swiss chard or spinach.

The best sauces for salads are invariably based on a green, quality extra-virgin olive oil and a little lemon juice or vinegar—what changes are the herbs that season them.

~~~~~~~~~~~~~~~~

Zeytinyağlı Salata Sosu

Olive Oil and Lemon Sauce

MAKES 1 1/2 CUPS

1/2 cup lemon juice
2 garlic cloves, minced
1 tablespoon dried or fresh oregano
1/3 cup coarsely chopped fresh Italian parsley leaves
 (optional)
1 cup extra-virgin olive oil
Salt and freshly ground black pepper

Combine the lemon juice, garlic, oregano, and parsley (if you're using it) in a small bowl. Slowly whisk in the olive oil. Season with salt and pepper. If the flavor is too strong, add a little cold water. Refrigerate the sauce for 20 minutes and whisk it just before serving.

~~~~~~~~~~~~~~~~

Yayla Salata Sosu

High Plateau Sauce

MAKES 1 1/2 CUPS

This sauce can also be served with cold cooked vegetables.

1/2 cup plain yogurt
2 garlic cloves, minced
1/4 cup coarsely chopped fresh mint
1/3 cup lemon juice
3/4 cup extra-virgin olive oil
Salt and freshly ground black pepper

Combine the yogurt, garlic, mint, and lemon juice in a small bowl. Slowly whisk in the olive oil. Season with salt and pepper. If the flavor is too strong, add a little cold water. Refrigerate the sauce for about 20 minutes and whisk it just before serving.

~~~~~~~~~~~~~~~~

Zeytinyağlı Sirkeli Salata Sosu

Olive Oil and Red Wine Vinegar Sauce

MAKES 1 1/2 CUPS

2 shallots, finely chopped
2 garlic cloves, minced
1 tablespoon dried oregano
1/2 cup red wine vinegar
1 cup extra-virgin olive oil
Salt and freshly ground black pepper
2 tablespoons finely chopped fresh Italian parsley

Combine the shallots, garlic, oregano, and red wine vinegar in a small bowl. Slowly whisk in the olive oil. Season with salt and pepper. Add the parsley. If the flavor is too strong, add a little cold water. Refrigerate the sauce for about 20 minutes and whisk it just before serving.

Ege Salata Sosu

Aegean Sauce

MAKES 2 CUPS

1 bunch watercress, trimmed and finely chopped
   (about 1 cup)
1/2 cup white wine vinegar
1/3 cup finely chopped pitted green olives
1 cup extra-virgin olive oil
Salt and freshly ground black pepper
4 ounces feta cheese, crumbled (1/2 cup)

To trim the watercress, remove the larger, bottom stems and keep the tender stems on the tip and the leaves.

Combine the watercress, white wine vinegar, and green olives in a small bowl. Slowly whisk in the olive oil. Season with salt and pepper. Add the feta cheese and stir well. If the flavor is too strong, add a little cold water. Refrigerate the sauce for about 20 minutes and whisk it just before serving.

Sarmısaklı Yoğurt Sos

Yogurt-Garlic Sauce

MAKES 1 2/3 CUPS

This popular sauce is traditionally served with grilled and stuffed vegetable dishes, pilafs, and böreks (savory pastries). It is also served with plain cooked greens, such as spinach or Swiss chard.

1 2/3 cups plain yogurt
4 garlic cloves, minced
Salt

In a small bowl, whisk the yogurt, garlic, and salt until the mixture is very smooth. Cover the bowl and refrigerate the sauce for at least 15 minutes to allow the flavor of the garlic to blend with the yogurt.

Beyaz Fıstıklı Tarator

Pine Nut Sauce

MAKES 1 2/3 CUPS

Serve this sauce with grilled meat and fish or as a dip for raw vegetables. It is also delicious made with chopped walnuts instead of the pine nuts.

1 slice day-old white bread, crusts removed
1 cup pine nuts
1 teaspoon minced garlic
1/2 cup lemon juice
1/2 cup extra-virgin olive oil
Salt

Soak the slice of bread in water briefly and squeeze out excess water.

Place the pine nuts, garlic, lemon juice, and bread in a food processor and process while slowly pouring in the olive oil. Add 2 tablespoons cold water and process until the mixture is smooth. Season with salt. Transfer the sauce to a bowl and refrigerate it for 1 hour before serving, to allow the flavors to blend.

Acı Kırmızı Biber Salçası

Red Hot Pepper Paste

MAKES 1 CUP

Use as a flavoring for soups, and serve with meats and fish.

    1 pound red chili peppers, cored and seeded
    1 pound red bell peppers, cored and seeded
    1 teaspoon sugar
    Salt
    2 tablespoons white wine vinegar
    2 tablespoons extra-virgin olive oil

Place the chili peppers and bell peppers in 1½ quarts boiling water and cook for 15 minutes, or until they're softened. Drain them and let them cool. Peel the skins from the peppers. Place them in a blender or food processor fitted with a metal blade and puree until smooth.

Transfer the puree to a saucepan over very low heat, add the sugar and season with salt. Simmer, uncovered, for about 25 minutes. Let the mixture cool to room temperature (about 1 hour). Pour it into a glass jar, add the vinegar, and stir. Pour the olive oil in gently so it stays in a layer on top of the pepper paste. Cover the jar and store it in the refrigerator. The paste will stay good refrigerated up to three months. Stir the paste before serving.

Terbiye

Egg and Lemon Sauce

MAKES 1½ CUPS

This sauce is served over stuffed grape leaves, stuffed swiss chard, and meat-stuffed vegetables (sarmas and dolmas).

    1½ cups chicken stock (page 58) or water
    4 egg yolks
    3 tablespoons lemon juice
    1 tablespoon cornstarch
    Salt

Slowly bring the chicken stock to a boil in a small saucepan. Meanwhile, in a small nonreactive bowl, combine the egg yolks, lemon juice, and cornstarch. Slowly whisk in this mixture to the boiling stock. Simmer for about 2 minutes until thickened. Serve warm over sarmas or dolmas.

Soğan Piyazı

Onion Relish

MAKES 1¾ CUPS

Serve this relish as an accompaniment to grilled meat or fish. Squeezing the sliced onions helps extract the juice so it blends with the other flavors.

    2 medium red onions, thinly sliced
    Salt
    2 teaspoons sumac
    2 teaspoons Turkish pepper or ground red pepper
    ½ cup coarsely chopped fresh Italian parsley leaves

Place the onion slices in a bowl, season with salt, and squeeze them a few times with your fingers to extract some of the juice. Add the sumac, Turkish red pepper, and parsley. Mix them together well.

~Clockwise from top: Pine Nut Sauce (page 13), Onion Relish (page 15), and Aegean Sauce (page 13)

MEZE APPETIZERS

~~~~~~~~~~~~~~~~~~~~~~~~

TURKISH CUISINE IS PERHAPS BEST known for its seemingly endless variety of hot and cold dishes that make up a *meze*. A meze (literally, "table") can be—and often is—served as an entire meal. It changes with the seasons and locale—according to what foods are available—but is constant in its abundance of choices. Fish restaurants along the coast serve specialty meze consisting of an array of seafood dishes prepared with squid, shrimp, octopus, mussels, or that most enticing of dishes—fresh sardines wrapped in grape leaves, which are eaten in late summer.

Seasonal vegetables are cooked in olive oil and flavored with herbs, a method called *zeytinyağlı*. *Dolmalar* (dolmas) are vegetables like peppers, artichokes, and eggplants, that are stuffed with rice, pine nuts, currants, and even meat. Leafy vegetables like grape leaves that are rolled around the stuffing are called *sarmalar* (sarmas). (Many people mistakenly call stuffed grape leaves dolmas.) Vegetable dishes in a meze are invariably served with Sarmısaklı Yoğurt Sos, a tangy yogurt-garlic sauce (page 13).

Eggplant, perhaps the most used vegetable in Turkish cuisine, is prepared in a number of ways for meze. Small eggplants stuffed with onion, garlic, tomato, and parsley make up the classic Imam Bayıldı. In Patlıcan Salatası, char-grilled eggplant is cut into pieces and mixed with tomatoes and grilled peppers. Patlıcan Ezmesi is a pureed eggplant dish—*ezmesi* means "pureed." Tomatoes, spinach, chickpeas, dried fava beans, and fava beans are also prepared this way.

A meze always includes sliced soft white cheese (*beyaz peynir*, which is like feta cheese), peeled and sliced ripe tomatoes, cucumbers, pistachios, fresh almonds, melons (when in season), and olives that are drizzled with olive oil and lemon juice and sprinkled with herbs. Fresh-baked bread is placed on the table, too. These dishes are traditionally enjoyed with the popular Turkish drink *rakı*—or "lion's milk" as it is often called—an anise-flavored liqueur that turns white when it is mixed with water.

What makes a meze such a good way to feed guests is that most of the food can be prepared a day in advance. Though a simple meze consists of as few as three dishes, for special occasions a selection of four or five vegetable dishes cooked in oil and stuffed vegetable dishes is arranged on the table alongside böreks, freshly baked bread, and tasty salads. Sometimes char-grilled fish or meat is also served.

~~~~~~~~~~~~~~~~~~~~~~~~~

Acılı Domates Ezmesi

Spicy Pureed Tomatoes

SERVES 4–6

This specialty of eastern Turkey is deep red and has a warm, rich flavor. If you do not find the color red enough, add a bit of tomato paste. Serve it with grilled meat, chicken, or fish.

> 4 large tomatoes, peeled, seeded and finely chopped (2½ cups)
> 3 scallions, trimmed and finely chopped, some green parts included
> 1 large cucumber, peeled, seeded, and finely chopped (1 cup)
> 2 Italian green peppers, finely diced (½ cup)
> 1 tablespoon dried mint
> ¼ cup finely chopped parsley
> 3 tablespoons virgin olive oil
> 2 tablespoons lemon juice
> 2 tablespoons white wine vinegar
> 4 garlic cloves, minced
> ¼ cup paprika
> 1 teaspoon freshly ground black pepper
> 3 teaspoons Turkish red pepper or ground red pepper
> Salt
> Pita bread

Place all the ingredients except the pita bread in a food processor fitted with a metal blade, and pulse two or three times, just long enough to make a finer consistency. Place the mixture in a shallow serving bowl, cover it, and refrigerate for 1 hour. Serve chilled or at room temperature with pita bread.

~~~~~~~~~~~~~~~~~~~~~~~~~

İmam Bayıldı (Swooning Imam)

Stuffed Eggplant

SERVES 6

The story is that when an imam came home from the mosque, his wife had prepared this dish for his lunch. On tasting it, he fainted. Some think it was because he was so delighted with the dish; others

~ Swooning Imam

think that his reaction was more due to the high cost of one of its main ingredients: olive oil.

> 6 Italian eggplants (about 2 pounds), each about 6 inches long
> ¾ cup virgin olive oil, divided
> 4 medium Spanish onions, thinly sliced (2 cups)
> 12 garlic cloves, finely chopped
> 2 large tomatoes, peeled and chopped (1½ cups)
> 1 bunch fresh Italian parsley, trimmed and coarsely chopped
> 2 teaspoons sugar
> Salt and freshly ground black pepper
> 1 cup light olive oil or vegetable oil
> 3 small Italian green peppers, seeded and cut in half

Heat the oven to 350°F.

Peel off half the eggplant skin on each eggplant in alternating lengthwise strips to create a striped effect—but leave the stems intact. Make a deep slit lengthwise along the center of each eggplant; *do not cut all the way through or all the way to the ends.* Place the eggplants in a bowl, sprinkle them generously with salt, and cover them with cold water. Let the eggplants soak for about 20 minutes.

Heat ½ cup of the virgin olive oil in a deep skillet over medium heat. Using a wooden spoon, stir in the onion, garlic, tomatoes, parsley, and sugar. Season with salt and pepper. Add ¼ cup cold water and stir the mixture well. Lower the heat, cover the skillet, and simmer for about 12 minutes, stirring occasionally, until the onions are softened but not brown. Uncover the skillet and let the mixture cool.

Rinse the eggplants under cold running water. Gently squeeze out the excess water and pat the eggplants dry with paper towels.

Heat 1 cup light olive oil or vegetable oil in another deep skillet. Fry the eggplants until they're lightly browned on both sides, then remove them from the skillet with a slotted spoon. Add the green peppers to the pan and fry them for about 2 minutes.

Place the eggplants side by side in a baking dish, open-side up. Sprinkle the insides of each eggplant with salt, then stuff each one with the onion mixture. Lay half a green pepper on top of each eggplant. Pour over ½ cup cold water and the remaining virgin olive oil. Cover the eggplant and peppers with parchment paper and bake for about 40 minutes. Let the dish cool, and serve at room temperature.

~~~~~~~~~~~~~~~~~~~~~~~~~

Patlıcan Biber Tavası Yoğurtlu Sarmısaklı ve Domates Soslu

Fried Eggplant and Green Peppers with Yogurt-Garlic and Tomato Sauces

SERVES 4–6

On summer afternoons almost every neighborhood is filled with the smells of eggplant and green peppers frying.

> 6 Italian eggplants (about 2 pounds)
> 4 tablespoons salt
> 6 medium Italian green peppers
> 2 cups light olive oil or vegetable oil
> 6 fresh Italian parsley sprigs
> 1 recipe Yogurt-Garlic Sauce (page 13)

TOMATO SAUCE
> 1 tablespoon virgin olive oil
> 3 garlic cloves, minced
> 2 large tomatoes, peeled, seeded, and finely chopped
> (1½ cups)

Cut the stems off the eggplants, then peel off half the skin in alternating lengthwise strips to create a striped effect. Cut the eggplants into ½-inch-thick slices crosswise or diagonally or lengthwise, so you have pieces of different shapes. Add the salt to 2 quarts cold water. Soak the eggplant slices in the salted water for 20 minutes.

Meanwhile, make the tomato sauce. Heat the olive oil in a small saucepan, and cook the garlic, stirring it with a wooden spoon, until it's softened but not brown, about 1 minute. Add the tomatoes, cover the saucepan, and cook gently for 2 more minutes. Set aside the sauce.

Remove the eggplant slices from the water with a slotted spoon, and pat them dry with paper towels. Dry the whole green peppers well also.

Heat 1 cup of the oil in a frying pan over medium heat. It is important that the oil be hot enough (about 350–365°F) so the eggplant does not become greasy. To test the hot oil, dip a piece of eggplant into the oil, taking care not to burn yourself—if the oil sizzles, it's ready. Fry the eggplant slices on both sides until they are light brown, about 2 minutes. Do not crowd them in the pan. Remove them from the oil and put them to drain on paper towels. Add more oil to the pan as needed.

When the eggplant is fried, add the whole green peppers to the pan and fry them until they're softened. Drain them on paper towels. Let the vegetables cool.

Arrange the eggplants and green peppers on a serving platter, garnish with sprigs of parsley, and serve with the tomato and yogurt-garlic sauces.

~~~~~~~~~~~~~~~~~~~~~~~~~

Patlıcan Ezmesi

Eggplant Puree with Olive Oil and Lemon Juice

SERVES 4–6

This dish is best when the eggplant is prepared over a charcoal grill, which gives it a characteristic smoky taste.

> 3 or 4 large globe eggplants (total weight about
> 4 pounds)
> 6 tablespoons lemon juice, divided
> 1 tablespoon salt, plus more to season
> ¼ cup virgin olive oil
> 4 garlic cloves, minced
> 4 sprigs fresh Italian parsley, coarsely chopped
> ½ cup mixed olives
> 2 tomatoes, quartered
> 1 small red onion, finely sliced
> Pita bread

Prepare a charcoal grill or heat the oven to 450°F. Using the tip of a skewer, poke 2-inch-deep holes all over the eggplants to allow the heat to get into the whole eggplant. Grill them over the charcoal fire, turning occasionally, for about 20 minutes, or until they completely collapse. Alternatively, place them in a baking pan and bake for about 40 minutes in the oven. Let them cool.

Mix 1 cup cold water, 3 tablespoons of the lemon juice, and 1 tablespoon salt and set the mixture aside.

When they're cool enough to handle, lay the eggplants on a cutting board and peel off the skin, starting from the stem and working downward. Discard the skin and stems. Add the eggplant pulp to the lemon mixture and set it aside for 10 minutes. (The lemon mixture helps prevent the eggplant from discoloring.)

Transfer the pulp to a strainer. Using the back of a wooden spoon, squeeze the excess liquid from the pulp. Return the eggplant pulp to the bowl, add the remaining lemon juice, the olive oil, and the garlic. Season with salt. Mash the mixture with a potato masher to make a smooth paste. Alternatively, place the eggplants in a food processor fitted with a metal blade and pulse a few times until smooth. Cover the bowl and refrigerate for at least 15 minutes.

Garnish with parsley, olives, tomatoes, and red onion slices. Serve with pita bread.

VARIATION

Yoğurtlu Patlıcan Ezmesi: Omit the 3 tablespoons of lemon juice and the olive oil used for seasoning. After you puree the eggplant, mix in 1½ cups Süzme Yogurt (page 36). Chill and serve.

~~~~~~~~~~~~~~~~~~~~~~~~~~

Patlıcan Salatası

Char-Grilled Eggplant Salad

SERVES 4–6

3 large eggplants (about 3 to 3⅓ pounds total)
6 tablespoons lemon juice, divided
1 tablespoon salt, plus extra to season
1 pound bell peppers (about 4 medium)
2 tomatoes, peeled, seeded, and chopped (1 cup)
4 garlic cloves, minced
¼ cup coarsely chopped fresh Italian parsley
¼ cup extra-virgin olive oil

Prepare a charcoal grill, or heat the oven to 450°F. Cook the eggplant the same way as for Patlıcan Ezmesi (page 20). Prepare the lemon juice mixture using 3 tablespoons of the lemon juice, mix the eggplant pulp with it, and set it aside for 10 minutes.

Grill the green peppers for 8 minutes, turning occasionally, until they blacken completely. If using the oven, cook them for 15 minutes. Place the peppers in a plastic bag for about 10 minutes so the skin loosens. Remove the tops, peel the skin, and chop them, taking care to remove the seeds.

Transfer the eggplant pulp to a strainer and squeeze out the excess liquid. Roughly chop the pulp and mix it with the green peppers, tomatoes, garlic, parsley, oil, and the remaining lemon juice. Season with salt. Stir gently, cover the bowl, and refrigerate for 30 minutes. Serve chilled.

~~~~~~~~~~~~~~~~~~~~~~~~~~

Zeytinyağlı Biber Dolması

Stuffed Green Peppers

SERVES 4–6

3 tablespoons currants
3 medium tomatoes
1 cup virgin olive oil
4 tablespoons pine nuts
1 medium Spanish onion, grated (1 cup)
1 cup long-grain rice
1½ teaspoons sugar
2 teaspoons ground cinnamon
2 tablespoons finely chopped fresh dill
¾ cup finely chopped fresh Italian parsley
Salt and freshly ground black pepper
12 small green bell peppers (about 3 pounds)
Lemon wedges, to garnish

Soak the currants in warm water for about 15–20 minutes. Meanwhile, peel, seed, and chop one of the tomatoes. Cut the other two tomatoes into 6 wedges each. Set the tomatoes aside.

Heat ½ cup of the olive oil in a medium-size pot over medium heat. Add the pine nuts and cook them for about 2 minutes, or until they're golden brown. Drain the currants and add them to the pot along with the onion, rice, sugar, cinnamon, and 2 cups hot water. Stir well, cover the pot, and cook the mixture over low heat for about 20 minutes, or until the water has been absorbed. The rice should be partially cooked.

Remove the pot from the heat, and stir in the chopped tomato, dill, and parsley. Season with salt and pepper. Set aside. Carefully cut off the tops of the green peppers and remove the seeds and cores. Fill each pepper with some of the rice mixture, pressing down gently and making sure not to overstuff it or it may burst during cooking. Place a tomato wedge over each stuffed pepper.

Stand the peppers side by side in a flameproof casserole dish. Pour over the remaining olive oil and 2 cups water. Cover the surface of the peppers with crumpled wet parchment paper. Place an ovenproof plate on top of the parchment paper (make sure it fits inside the pan) to weigh it down. Bring the mixture to a boil, then lower the heat, cover the dish, and simmer for about 55 minutes, or until the peppers are soft and the water has been absorbed. Let the peppers cool. Serve at room temperature garnished with lemon wedges.

Zeytinyağlı Yaprak Sarması (Yalancı)

Grape Leaves Stuffed with Rice, Pine Nuts, and Currants

SERVES 4–6

This is a popular summer meze along the Aegean Coast and the Mediterranean coast of Turkey. These stuffed grape leaves are very good served with a squeeze of fresh lemon juice.

This recipe is called *yalancı*, which means "fake," because the rice, pine nuts, and currants are substitutes for meat in the stuffing.

1 (16-ounce) jar grape leaves, drained
1/4 cup virgin olive oil
2 tablespoons lemon juice
Lemon wedges
Tomato wedges
Chopped fresh Italian parsley

STUFFING
3 tablespoons currants
2 tablespoons virgin olive oil
3 tablespoons pine nuts
1 small Spanish onion, finely chopped (1/2 cup)
1 cup long-grain white rice
1 tablespoon sugar
1 1/2 teaspoons ground cinnamon
2 cups hot water
2 tablespoons finely chopped fresh dill
2 tablespoons finely chopped fresh parsley
Salt and freshly ground black pepper

Soak the currants in warm water for about 15–20 minutes. Drain them and set them aside.

To prepare the grape leaves, bring 2 quarts water to a boil, unroll the grape leaves, and place them in the boiling water for 2 minutes to soften the leaves and rid them of the brine. Using a slotted spoon, remove the leaves from the water and drape them over the edge of a colander to drain. With a sharp knife, cut out the small protruding stem from each leaf. Set the grape leaves aside.

To make the stuffing heat the olive oil in a medium saucepan over medium heat, and cook the pine nuts for about 2 minutes, until they're golden brown. Add the currants, onion, rice, sugar, cinnamon, and 2 cups hot water. Stir the mixture, cover the pot, and cook gently for about 20 minutes, or until the water has been absorbed. Remove the pan from the heat and mix in the dill and parsley. Season to taste with salt and pepper. Let the stuffing cool for 30–40 minutes.

Preheat the oven to 350°F. To assemble the sarmas, line up 36 of the grape leaves side by side, vein side up and with the notch where you removed the stem closest to you. Place one tablespoon of the stuffing at the end of the leaf close to you. Fold the end nearest to you over the filling, then fold both sides of the leaf over the filling. Roll up the leaves—but not too tightly or they may burst.

Line a flameproof casserole dish with half the remaining grape leaves. Arrange the sarmas on top of the leaves, seam-side down. Pour 2 cups hot water, the olive oil, and the lemon juice over them. Cover the sarmas with the remaining grape leaves. Place crumpled wet parchment paper over the grape leaves, and weigh it down with an ovenproof plate (one small enough to fit inside the dish). Cover the dish, and on the stovetop over medium heat bring the liquid to a boil (about 5 minutes). Move the dish to the oven and cook gently for about 45 minutes, or until the sarmas are tender and the water has been absorbed.

Transfer the sarmas to a serving dish. Cover them and refrigerate. Serve chilled. Garnish with lemon wedges, tomatoes, and chopped parsley.

~ *Clockwise from top right:* Pureed Fish Roe (page 35), Fresh Fava Beans Cooked with Olive Oil (page 29), Grape Leaves Stuffed with Rice, Pine Nuts, and Currants, and an assortment of olives

~~~~~~~~~~~~~~~~~~~~

Zeytinyağlı Yerelması

Jerusalem Artichokes Cooked in Olive Oil

SERVES 4–6

Jerusalem artichoke is a root vegetable that looks similar to ginger-root, although the flavor is very different—nutty and a bit like artichoke. It has beige to light brownish-red skin and white to beige flesh. This winter dish is from the western part of Turkey.

1½ pounds Jerusalem artichokes
2 lemons, cut in half
¼ cup virgin olive oil
1 small Spanish onion, finely diced (½ cup)
1 carrot, sliced
¼ cup long-grain rice
2 teaspoons sugar
2 tablespoons lemon juice
3 tablespoons coarsely chopped fresh dill
Salt
Chopped parsley
Lemon wedges

Peel the artichokes and cut each one into 2 to 4 pieces depending on their size. Rub the pieces with the cut lemon halves and place them in a bowl of cold water to prevent discoloration.

Heat the oil in a large saucepan over medium heat and cook the onion gently until it's softened but not brown. Add the sliced carrot and cook for 1 minute. Drain the artichokes and add them to the pan along with the rice, sugar, lemon juice, and dill. Season with salt. Stir the mixture well.

Pour in 2 cups water, cover the pan, and cook gently for about 30 minutes, or until the Jerusalem artichokes are tender. Add a little hot water if the mixture gets dry before the artichokes finish cooking. Transfer the mixture to a serving plate and let it cool. Serve at room temperature with a garnish of chopped parsley and lemon wedges.

~~~~~~~~~~~~~~~~~~~~

Zeytinyağlı Kereviz

Celeriac with Vegetables in Olive Oil

SERVES 4–6

Celeriac is a root vegetable that has white to light brown skin and white flesh. When shopping, choose firm heavy ones. This winter dish is served as a meze or as a side dish.

4 celeriac knobs, peeled
1 lemon, cut in half
½ cup virgin olive oil
12 small shallots, peeled
2 carrots, diced (¾ cup)
2 potatoes, diced (¾ cup)
¾ cup green peas
2 teaspoons sugar
2 tablespoons chopped fresh dill
Salt and freshly ground black pepper
1 tablespoon flour
2 tablespoons chopped fresh Italian parsley
Lemon wedges

Cut off the ends of the celeriacs. Cut the celeriacs in half and scrape off the soft pulp in the middle. Rub the celeriacs with half of the lemon, and cook them in a large pot of boiling water for about 15 minutes or until they're tender. Drain them and cut them into ½-inch-thick slices. Set the celeriacs aside.

Heat the olive oil in a large saucepan over medium heat, and cook the shallots for about 2 minutes until soft but not brown. Add the carrots, potatoes, green peas, and 4 cups water, and bring the mixture to a boil. Lower the heat, cover the pan, and cook for 10 minutes. Add the celeriac, sugar, the juice of the remaining half lemon, and the dill, and mix well. Season with salt and pepper.

Blend the flour with 2 tablespoons water and stir it into the vegetable mixture. Cook for another 10 minutes, until the vegetables are tender and the cooking liquid has thickened slightly. Add a little water if the mixture gets dry during cooking.

Transfer the celeriac slices to a serving platter with a slotted spoon, arranging them in a circular pattern. Place the vegetable mixture in the center and pour the thickened cooking liquid over it. Cover the platter and refrigerate for an hour. Serve at room temperature or chilled, with a garnish of chopped parsley and lemon wedges.

~~~~~~~~~~~~~~~~~~~~~~~

Zeytinyağlı Pırasa

Leeks in Olive Oil

SERVES 4–6

> 2 pounds leeks
> 1/4 cup virgin olive oil
> 1 small Spanish onion, finely chopped (1/2 cup)
> 2 carrots, sliced (3/4 cup)
> 1/2 cup long-grain rice
> 1/2 cup finely chopped fresh Italian parsley
> 2 teaspoons sugar
> 2 tablespoons lemon juice
> Salt

Cut off the roots and about two thirds of the green part of the leeks. Remove the coarse outer leaves. Slice the leeks 1-inch deep lengthwise and split them open. Wash them well, removing all traces of dirt. Cut the leeks into 1/2-inch-wide slices and set them aside.

Heat the oil in a large saucepan over medium heat, and cook the onion gently for about 2 minutes, or until it's softened but not brown. Add the leeks, carrots, rice, parsley, sugar, and lemon juice. Season with salt and stir the mixture. Pour in 2 cups hot water, cover the pan, and cook gently for about 20 minutes, or until the leeks are tender.

Transfer the mixture to a serving dish, cover, and refrigerate for 1 hour. Serve chilled or at room temperature.

~~~~~~~~~~~~~~~~~~~~~~~

Ispanaklı Yoğurt Ezmesi

Spicy Spinach Puree with Thick Yogurt

SERVES 4–6

> 1 1/2 pounds fresh spinach, washed and trimmed
> 4 garlic cloves, minced
> 2 teaspoons Turkish red pepper or ground red pepper
> 1/4 cup virgin olive oil
> 2 cups Thick Yogurt Spread (page 36)
> Salt
> Paprika
> Assorted olives
> Toasted pita bread

Place the spinach in a saucepan with 1 quart water and bring to a boil. Cook the spinach for 2 minutes, then drain it, squeezing out the excess liquid. Chop the spinach finely. Place it in a bowl and add the garlic, Turkish red pepper, olive oil, and thick yogurt spread. Season with salt. Stir the mixture gently with a wooden spoon, cover the bowl, and refrigerate for one hour. Garnish with paprika and olives. Serve with toasted pita bread.

~~~~~~~~~~~~~~~~~~~~~~~

Ispanak Kavurma

Sautéed Spinach with Yogurt-Garlic Sauce

SERVES 4–6

This simple, colorful dish is especially good with grilled meat, or chicken.

> 1 1/2 pounds fresh spinach, washed and trimmed
> 1 tablespoon virgin olive oil
> 4 teaspoons clarified butter (page 7), divided
> 1 small Spanish onion, finely chopped (1/2 cup)
> 2 garlic cloves, minced
> 1 large tomato, peeled, seeded, and diced (3/4 cup)
> 2 teaspoons salt
> 2 teaspoons Turkish red pepper or ground red pepper, divided
> 2 teaspoons paprika, divided
> 1 recipe Yogurt-Garlic Sauce (page 13), to serve

In a large saucepan, bring 2 cups water to a boil and cook the spinach for about 2 minutes. Drain the spinach, reserving 1/2 cup of the cooking liquid. Squeeze out the excess liquid and chop the spinach finely.

Heat the oil and 2 teaspoons of the butter in a medium-size saucepan over medium heat. Add the onion, and cook gently until it's softened but not brown, about 2 minutes. Add the spinach, garlic, tomato, salt, 1 teaspoon of the Turkish red pepper, and 1 teaspoon of the paprika. Stir in the reserved 1/2 cup spinach liquid, then remove the saucepan from the heat. Transfer this mixture to a serving plate and let it cool.

Pour the yogurt-garlic sauce over the cooled spinach mixture. Heat the remaining 2 teaspoons butter in a small saucepan, stir in the remaining Turkish red pepper and paprika. Drizzle this butter mixture over the yogurt-garlic sauce, and serve at once.

~~~~~~~~~~~~~~~~~~~~~~

Zeytinyağlı Enginar Dolması

**Rice-and-Herb-Stuffed Artichokes with
Fava Beans and Olive Oil**

SERVES 4–6

This recipe comes from my hometown of İzmir, but it is also prepared in the western and Mediterranean regions of Turkey. It is
usually eaten in the summer when artichokes are harvested.

This dish can be cooked entirely on the stovetop, but finishing it
in the oven allows it to cook more evenly. Traditionally, Turkish
homes didn't have stoves, so people cooked dishes like these over a
paraffin burner or in a brick oven.

1/4 cup flour
1/2 cup lemon juice, divided
6 medium or 12 small artichokes (about 21/2 pounds)
2 lemons, cut in half
2 large carrots
3/4 cup virgin olive oil, divided
1/2 cup short-grain rice
3 scallions, trimmed and finely chopped,
    some green parts included
1/2 cup finely chopped fresh dill, divided
1/2 cup finely chopped Italian parsley, divided
1 tablespoon sugar
1/2 cup shelled fresh fava beans
Salt and freshly ground black pepper
Sprigs of fresh dill
Lemon wedges

To prepare the artichokes, mix the flour and 1/4 cup of the
lemon juice with 2 quarts cold water in a large bowl. Cut off the
stems so the artichokes can stand, and trim the bottoms. Remove
any hard outer leaves, trim off tough upper edges, and scoop out
the choke, scraping it out thoroughly. Rub the artichokes all over
with the cut lemon halves and place the artichokes in the flour and
water mixture to help prevent discoloration.

Cut and shape the carrots into 11/2-inch ovals, shaped like
large olives (see photograph, opposite).

Preheat the oven to 350°F. For the stuffing, heat 1/2 cup of
the olive oil in a medium saucepan. Add the rice, scallions, 1/4 cup
of the dill, 1/4 cup of the parsley, sugar, and 1 cup of the water,
stirring to combine them. Bring the mixture to a boil, then lower
the heat, cover the pan, and cook over low heat for about 10 minutes, or until the water has been absorbed.

Remove the artichokes from the water and shake off the excess water. Stuff the artichokes with the rice mixture, pressing down
gently to pack it in a bit. Do not overstuff them. Place them in a
flameproof casserole dish upright, side by side.

Add the fava beans and carrots to the casserole dish. Pour
over the remaining 1/4 cup olive oil, the remaining 1/4 cup lemon
juice, 1 cup water, and the remaining dill and parsley. Lay a crumpled piece of wet parchment paper directly on top of the artichokes, and weigh it down with an ovenproof plate (one small
enough to fit inside the dish). On the stovetop, over medium heat,
bring the liquid to a boil. Once it has boiled, cover the dish and
move it to the oven. Cook gently for about 40–45 minutes, or until
most of the liquid has been absorbed and the artichokes are tender.
Let the dish cool.

Transfer the artichokes with fava beans and carrots to a serving dish, spooning the cooking juices on top. Serve chilled or at
room temperature. Garnish with sprigs of dill and lemon wedges.
NOTE: If fresh fava beans are unavailable, use fresh green peas.

~ Rice-and-Herb-Stuffed Artichokes with Fava Beans
and Olive Oil

~~~~~~~~~~~~~~~~~~~~

Tahanlı Nohut Ezmesi (Humus)

Hummus (Pureed Chickpeas with Tahini)

SERVES 4–6

I developed this version of hummus myself. It was a "Hit of the Week" in the *Boston Globe* in 1986 and has been a favorite dish at Sultan's Kitchen for many years.

In the eastern part of Turkey hummus is served hot rather than cold. For a variation, serve it topped with roasted pine nuts or walnuts and with a drizzle of hot clarified butter mixed with some Turkish hot pepper.

1 1/2 cups dried chickpeas, soaked overnight (page 7)
2 teaspoons salt and a little more to season
3 garlic cloves, chopped
1/2 cup lemon juice
1/4 cup virgin olive oil
1/4 cup tahini
Sliced red onion
Assorted olives
Paprika
Toasted pita bread

Place the chickpeas in a medium-size saucepan with 2 1/2 cups of water and 2 teaspoons of salt. Bring the chickpeas to a boil, lower the heat, and simmer for about 1 1/2 hours, or until they are tender. Add more water if it is absorbed too quickly. Drain the chickpeas and reserve 1/2 cup of the cooking liquid. Set aside.

In a food processor fitted with a metal blade, process the chickpeas, garlic, lemon juice, olive oil, and the reserved cooking liquid until the mixture is smooth. Season with salt. Transfer the mixture to a bowl and stir in the tahini to make a smooth paste. Garnish with sliced red onion and olives and sprinkle with paprika. Serve with toasted pita bread.

~~~~~~~~~~~~~~~~~~~~

Zeytinyağlı Kuru Fasülye Pilakisi

Lima Beans with Vegetables and Olive Oil

SERVES 4–6

1 pound dried medium or large lima beans (2 cups),
    soaked overnight (page 7)
1/2 cup virgin olive oil
1 small Spanish onion, finely diced (1/2 cup)
4 garlic cloves, minced
1 tablespoon tomato paste
2 carrots, diced (3/4 cup)
1 rib celery, diced (1/2 cup)
2 potatoes, diced (3/4 cup)
2 tablespoons lemon juice
Salt and freshly ground black pepper
3 tablespoons coarsely chopped fresh Italian parsley
Lemon wedges

Drain the soaked beans, place them in a saucepan, and cover them with cold water. Bring the water to a boil, then lower the heat, cover the pan, and cook the beans gently for about 30 minutes, or until they're just tender.

Meanwhile, heat the olive oil in a large saucepan over medium heat, and cook the onion gently for about 2 minutes, until it's softened but not brown. Stir in the garlic, tomato paste, carrots, and celery. Drain the cooked beans and add them to the pan, cover it, and simmer for about 15 minutes. Add the potatoes and lemon juice. Season with salt and pepper, cover the pan, and simmer for another 10 minutes, or until the vegetables are tender.

Transfer the vegetable mixture to a serving dish, cover it and refrigerate if for 1 hour. Serve chilled or at room temperature, garnished with parsley and lemon wedges.

Zeytinyağlı Taze Bakla
Fresh Fava Beans Cooked with Olive Oil
SERVES 4–6

This recipe, in which the entire fava pod and beans are eaten, comes from the Aegean region. It is prepared in the southern and western parts of the country in early spring and summer, when fava beans are young and tender. The dish is delicious served on hot days with Yogurt-Garlic Sauce or just plain yogurt.

> 1¹/₂ pounds fresh fava beans
> 2 tablespoons all-purpose flour
> 1 tablespoon lemon juice
> ¹/₂ cup virgin olive oil
> 1 small Spanish onion, finely diced (¹/₂ cup)
> 3 tablespoons coarsely chopped fresh dill
> Salt
> 1 recipe Yogurt-Garlic Sauce (page 13)

Prepare the beans by snapping off one end and pulling off the string, then turning the beans over and pulling the strings from the other side. Cut the fava beans in half and place them in a bowl. Cover them with cold water, sprinkle on the flour, and stir in the lemon juice. Set aside.

Heat the olive oil in a deep pot over medium heat and cook the onion gently for about 2 minutes, until it's softened but not brown. Drain the beans and add them to the pot along with 2 tablespoons of the dill and 1¹/₂ cups water. Season with salt. Bring the mixture to a boil, then lower the heat, cover the pot, and simmer for about 40 minutes, or until the beans are tender.

Transfer the mixture to a serving platter, cover it, and refrigerate. Pour the yogurt-garlic sauce over the beans and sprinkle on the rest of the chopped dill. Serve chilled or at room temperature.

Zeytinyağlı Taze Fasülye
Green Beans with Tomatoes and Olive Oil
SERVES 4–6

You can use any type of green beans, long or short, round or flat, for this recipe. In Turkey, flat green beans that don't have strings are used. When buying string beans, look for fresh, bright green beans that snap sharply when broken in two.

> ¹/₂ cup virgin olive oil
> 1 small Spanish onion, finely diced (¹/₂ cup)
> 2 garlic cloves, minced
> 2 tomatoes, peeled, seeded, and finely diced (¹/₂ cup)
> 1¹/₂ pounds fresh green beans, trimmed and cut
>   in half lengthwise
> Salt and freshly ground black pepper
> 3 tablespoons chopped fresh Italian parsley

Heat the oil in a medium-size pot over medium heat and cook the onion gently for about 2 minutes, or until it's softened but not brown. Stir in the garlic, tomato, and beans. Season with salt and pepper. Add 1¹/₂ cups water and bring the mixture to a boil; then lower the heat, cover the pot, and simmer gently for about 35 minutes, or until the beans are tender but not too soft.

Transfer the mixture to a serving plate, cover it, and refrigerate for 1 hour. Serve chilled or at room temperature with a garnish of chopped parsley.

~ *Above:* Fresh Fava Beans Cooked with Olive Oil and served with Yogurt-Garlic Sauce (page 13)

~~~~~~~~~~~~~~~~~~~~~~

Çerkez Tavuğu

Circassian Chicken

SERVES 4–6

This dish is one of the classical masterpieces of Turkish cuisine and is served on special occasions. Traditionally the walnuts were crushed between two stones, and the walnut oil was collected and drizzled over the dish. Use only the best-quality paprika and make sure that the walnuts are sweet. Though it won't give the same flavor, olive oil may be used instead of the walnut oil.

    2 pounds boneless, skinless chicken breasts
    3 cups chicken stock (page 58)
    2 tablespoons walnut oil or extra-virgin olive oil
    2 teaspoons paprika
    2 tablespoons coarsely chopped fresh Italian parsley
    Walnut halves

WALNUT SAUCE
    2 slices day-old white bread, crusts removed
    2 tablespoons unsalted clarified butter (page 7)
    1 small Spanish onion, finely chopped (1/2 cup)
    2 garlic cloves, minced
    1 1/2 tablespoons paprika
    1 teaspoon ground red pepper
    1 1/2 cups chopped walnuts
    Salt

Place the chicken breasts and the chicken stock in a saucepan, cover it, and bring the liquid to a boil. Lower the heat and simmer gently for 15 minutes, or until the chicken is cooked. (Be careful not to overcook the chicken, or it will lose some of its flavor.) Using a slotted spoon, remove the chicken and let it cool. Reserve about 2 cups of the cooking liquid and keep the rest for another use.

To make the walnut sauce, soak the bread in a little of the reserved chicken stock, then squeeze it dry and crumble it into a small bowl. Set the bread aside. In a small saucepan, heat the clarified butter over medium heat, add the onion, and cook gently for about 2 minutes until the onion is softened but not brown. Stir in the garlic, paprika, and ground red pepper. Remove the saucepan from the heat and set the mixture aside.

In a food processor or blender, finely grind the walnuts. Add 1 cup of the reserved cooking liquid, the onion mixture, and crumbled bread. Season with salt and blend well to make a smooth sauce. If the sauce is too thick, add a little more of the reserved cooking liquid.

Using a sharp knife, shred the chicken and place the pieces in a large bowl. Add the sauce and mix well. Transfer the mixture to a serving platter.

To prepare the garnish, warm the walnut oil in a small saucepan and stir in the paprika. Drizzle this sauce over the shredded chicken mixture. Sprinkle with chopped parsley and decorate with the walnut halves.

~~~~~~~~~~~~~~~~~~~~~~

Kuru Bakla Ezmesi (Fava)

Pureed Dried Fava Beans

SERVES 4–6

    1 pound dried fava (or broad) beans (2 cups),
        soaked overnight (page 7)
    1 small Spanish onion, chopped (1/2 cup)
    2 teaspoons salt
    1/4 cup extra-virgin olive oil
    2 tablespoons lemon juice
    1 red onion, thinly sliced
    Finely chopped fresh Italian parsley
    Paprika
    Toasted triangles of pita bread

Drain the soaked beans and remove the skins. Place them in a medium-size pot along with the onion, 3 1/2 cups water, and the salt. Bring the mixture to a boil, then lower the heat, cover the pot, and simmer for about 1 hour, or until the beans are well cooked and the water has been absorbed.

Transfer the bean mixture to a food processor fitted with a metal blade. Process until the mixture is smooth. If it seems too thick, add a little water and continue processing.

Spread the puree in a shallow dish, cover it, and refrigerate for an hour, or until it is fully set—it should be solid, not soft or runny. Cut the fava spread into several pieces and drizzle them with olive oil and lemon juice. Garnish with the red onion slices, and sprinkle with parsley and paprika. Serve with the pita toasts.

~ *Clockwise from top right:* Circassian Chicken (page 30), Fried Eggplant and Green Peppers with Yogurt-Garlic and Tomato Sauce (page 20), and Zucchini Fritters (page 33)

~~~~~~~~~~~~~~~~~~~~~~~~

Zeytinyağlı Barbunya
Fasülye Pilakisi

Roman Beans with Vegetables and Olive Oil

SERVES 4–6

This way of preparing beans with vegetables and olive oil is called
pilaki and is from western Turkey. This dish can be served as a
meze, or it can accompany grilled meat and chicken.

13/4 pound dried Roman, cranberry, or pinto beans
    (21/2 cups), soaked overnight (page 7)
1/2 cup virgin olive oil
1 small Spanish onion, finely diced (1/2 cup)
4 garlic cloves, minced
1 tablespoon tomato paste
2 carrots, diced (3/4 cup)
1 rib celery, diced (1/2 cup)
2 potatoes, diced (3/4 cup)
2 tablespoons lemon juice
Salt and freshly ground black pepper
2 tablespoons coarsely chopped fresh Italian parsley
Lemon wedges

Drain the beans. Cook them in a large pot with 4 cups of water for about 1 hour, or until they are not quite tender. Set them
aside.

Heat the olive oil in a large pot over medium heat, and cook
the onion gently for about 2 minutes, or until it's softened but not
brown. Stir in the garlic, tomato paste, carrots, and celery. Drain
the cooked beans and add them to the pot, cover it, and simmer
for about 15 minutes. Add the potatoes and lemon juice. Season
with salt and pepper. Cover the pot and simmer for another 10
minutes, or until the vegetables are tender.

Transfer the mixture to a serving dish, cover it, and refrigerate
for 1 hour. Serve chilled or at room temperature with a garnish of
chopped parsley and lemon wedges.

~~~~~~~~~~~~~~~~~~~~~~~~

Mercimek Köftesi

Lentil and Bulgur Patties

SERVES 4–6

This recipe is prepared all over Turkey, although the seasonings vary
slightly from region to region.

2 tablespoons virgin olive oil
1 small Spanish onion, finely chopped (1/2 cup)
1 pound red lentils, rinsed and drained (2 cups)
11/2 tablespoons tomato paste
1 cup bulgur
4 scallions, trimmed and finely chopped, some green
    parts included
2 teaspoons Turkish red pepper or ground red pepper
1 tablespoon ground cumin
1 tablespoon dried mint
1/2 cup finely chopped fresh Italian parsley
Salt and freshly ground black pepper
Lemon wedges
1 recipe Yogurt-Garlic Sauce (page 13),

Heat the olive oil in a large pot over medium heat. Add the
onion and cook gently until it's softened but not brown. Add the
red lentils, tomato paste, and 3 cups water. Stir, cover the pot, and
bring the mixture to a boil. Lower the heat, add the bulgur, and
simmer with the pot covered for 25 minutes, or until the lentils are
tender.

Remove the pot from the heat. Reserve about 2 tablespoons of
the chopped scallions for garnish and add the rest to the pot along
with the Turkish hot red pepper, cumin, mint, and parsley. Season
with salt and pepper and mix well. Let the mixture cool at room
temperature for about 15 minutes.

Form the mixture into small oval shapes, using about 1 tablespoon of mixture for each. Place the ovals on a serving plate and
refrigerate them for 30 minutes.

Garnish with lemon wedges and the reserved scallions. Serve at
room temperature with yogurt-garlic sauce.

~~~~~~~~~~~~~~~~~~~~~~~~

Kabak Mücveri

Zucchini Fritters

SERVES 4–6

1½ pounds small, firm zucchini, grated (4 cups)
1 bunch scallions, trimmed and finely chopped,
    white parts only (½ cup)
2 tablespoons finely chopped fresh dill
2 tablespoons finely chopped fresh Italian parsley
3 eggs
1 tablespoon paprika
Salt and freshly ground black pepper
8 ounces crumbled feta cheese (1 cup)
1 cup all-purpose flour
1½ cups light olive oil or vegetable oil
1 recipe Yogurt-Garlic Sauce (page 13) (optional)

Place the grated zucchini in a colander, sprinkle it with salt and let it drain for about 15 minutes. Squeeze out the excess juice and place the zucchini in a large bowl together with the scallions, dill, parsley, eggs, and paprika, mixing well. Season with salt and pepper. Stir in the feta cheese and flour a little at a time and incorporate them well.

Heat the oil in a skillet, then lower the heat to medium. Scoop out tablespoonfuls of the zucchini mixture and gently drop them into the hot oil. Make sure you do not crowd the fritters in the skillet. Fry them all over until they're golden brown, about 5 minutes. Drain the fritters on paper towels. Serve them at once. Alternatively, serve them at room temperature with yogurt-garlic sauce.

~~~~~~~~~~~~~~~~~~~~~~~~

Balık Köftesi

Fish Patties

SERVES 4–6

1 quart fish stock (page 60)
1 pound haddock or other firm white fish
2 slices day-old white bread
2 eggs
1 bunch scallions, trimmed and finely chopped,
    some green parts included (½ cup)
¼ cup finely chopped fresh dill
¼ cup finely chopped fresh Italian parsley
Salt and freshly ground pepper
1½ cups light olive oil or vegetable oil
1 cup flour

Heat the fish stock to boiling, and poach the fish for about 5 minutes. It should not be completely cooked. Remove the fish from the pan with a slotted spoon, let it cool a little, and then cut it into small pieces, taking care to remove any bones. Save the cooking liquid for another use, such as fish soup.

Soak the bread slices in a little water for a few minutes, then squeeze out the excess liquid. Crumble the bread into a bowl. Add the fish, eggs, scallions, dill, and parsley. Season with salt and pepper. Mix well.

Heat the oil in a skillet, and then lower the heat to medium. Shape 1 tablespoon of the fish mixture into a flat oval and roll it in the flour. Repeat the procedure with half of the fish mixture. Drop the patties into the hot oil, without crowding them in the pan, and fry them on both sides until they're golden brown, about 5 minutes. Place them on paper towels to drain. Shape the rest of the fish mixture into patties, fry them, and drain them on paper towels. Serve hot or at room temperature.

~~~~~~~~~~~~~~~~~~~~~~~~~~~

Kalamar Tavası

Pan-Fried Squid

SERVES 4–6

 2 pounds squid, cleaned and cut into ¼-inch rings
 2 cups all-purpose flour
 Salt
 1 cup light olive oil or vegetable oil
 2 tablespoons clarified butter (page 7)
 2 tablespoons lemon juice
 ¼ cup dry white wine
 1 lemon, cut into wedges
 1 tablespoon coarsely chopped fresh Italian parsley

To clean the squid, wash it in cold water, remove the tentacles and the head, peel back and remove the skin from the hood, and rinse it again in cold water. Cut the white flesh into ¼-inch rings.

Season the flour with salt. Working in batches, coat the squid with the flour. Place the squid rings in a sieve and shake them to remove the excess flour.

Heat the oil in a large pan over high heat. Fry the squid until it's golden brown, about 2 minutes—do not overcrowd the pan while frying. Drain the squid briefly on paper towels. The next two steps should be done quickly so the squid stays crispy.

Heat the clarified butter in a large skillet over high heat and add the fried squid. While shaking this pan over the heat, add the lemon juice and white wine. Toss the mixture together quickly and remove the squid from the pan. Garnish with lemon wedges and chopped parsley. Serve immediately.

~~~~~~~~~~~~~~~~~~~~~~~

Cacık

Cucumbers with Yogurt and Mint

SERVES 4–6

This light and refreshing cucumber dish can be served as a meze on a hot summer day, or it can be served with grilled meats, böreks, and pilafs.

 5 cups plain yogurt
 4 garlic cloves, minced
 2 teaspoons salt

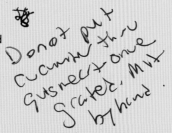

 1 tablespoon dried mint
 3 cucumbers, peeled, seeded, and grated or finely
   diced (2½ cups)
 8–10 fresh mint leaves
 Extra-virgin olive oil

Beat together the yogurt, garlic, and salt until smooth. Add the dried mint, cucumber, and 1 cup cold water and mix well. Pour the mixture into individual serving bowls. Garnish with fresh mint leaves and a few drops of olive oil. Cover and refrigerate at least 1 hour. Serve very cold.

~~~~~~~~~~~~~~~~~~~~~~~~~~~

Süzme Yoğurt Ezmesi (Haydari)

Thick Yogurt Spread

MAKES 2 CUPS

Yogurt that is drained this way—in Turkey it is done by hanging a cloth bundle of yogurt from a hook—is also called *torba yoğurdu* or "sack yogurt." It keeps well in the refrigerator for up to one week.

 6 cups plain yogurt
 3 garlic cloves, minced
 2 teaspoons Turkish red pepper or ground red pepper
 1 tablespoon finely chopped fresh dill
 Salt
 ½ teaspoon paprika
 Extra-virgin olive oil, to drizzle
 Toasted pita bread

Line a large sieve with a double thickness of cheesecloth and place the sieve over a large bowl. Pour the yogurt into the sieve and loosely cover it with parchment paper. Let the yogurt drain overnight.

Transfer the yogurt to a bowl, and add the garlic, Turkish red pepper, and dill. Season with salt. Stir the yogurt gently with a wooden spoon until it's smooth and creamy. Cover the bowl and refrigerate for at least 20 minutes before serving. Garnish with a drizzle of olive oil and sprinkle with paprika. Serve with toasted pita bread.

Beyaz Peynir Ezmesi

Spicy Pureed Feta Cheese

SERVES 4–6

1 pound feta cheese, broken into chunks
4 garlic cloves, minced
2 teaspoons paprika
2 teaspoons Turkish red pepper or ground red pepper
3 tablespoons extra-virgin olive oil, plus extra for
    drizzling
2 teaspoons dried mint
Sliced tomatoes
Assorted olives

Soak the feta cheese in warm water for about 30 minutes, changing the water often. Doing so will reduce the saltiness of the cheese. Drain the cheese well, then crumble it.

Place the feta cheese, garlic, paprika, Turkish red pepper, and olive oil in a food processor fitted with a metal blade. Process the mixture until smooth. Transfer it to a shallow bowl, cover, and refrigerate for at least 20 minutes.

Serve the cheese at room temperature. Drizzle olive oil over the top and sprinkle with the dried mint. Serve with sliced tomatoes and assorted olives.

Sigara ve Nuska Böreği

Cigar- and Triangle-Shaped Pastries

SERVES 4–6

These crispy böreks are always part of a meze and are also served as a snack with Turkish tea or ayran. In Turkey they are made with a dough called *yufka.* You can use ready-made filo dough, make your own (see page 136 for the recipe), or purchase it through mail order.

12 ounces crumbled feta cheese (1¹/₂ cups)
2 eggs
4 sprigs finely chopped fresh Italian parsley
2 scallions, trimmed and finely chopped
1 pound filo dough, about 20 to 22 sheets
2 cups light olive oil or other vegetable oil for frying
1 recipe Yogurt-Garlic Sauce (page 13) or plain yogurt
    (optional)

In a bowl, mix the feta cheese, eggs, parsley, and scallions. Set the mixture aside.

Unroll one sheet of the filo dough onto a flat surface. Keep the remaining dough covered with a damp towel to help prevent it from drying out. Using a sharp knife, cut the sheet of dough lengthwise into 4 equal strips. Working with one strip at a time, place 2 teaspoons of the feta cheese mixture near one end of the strip, then fold the strip into a triangle shape the way you fold up a flag: first fold the ends and sides of the dough in toward the center about ¹/₂ inch along each edge, then take the corner of the dough (at the filling end) and fold it diagonally so that it meets the opposite edge of pastry, forming a triangle; fold this triangle straight over to form a second triangle. Continue folding triangles down the entire strip of filo. Moisten the end of the dough with a little water and stick it to the triangle. Cover the stuffed and folded triangles with a damp towel to help prevent the dough from drying out; if you do this, the triangles will puff up more when you fry them. Continue making triangle-shaped pastries in the same way, using about 10 sheets of filo dough.

With the remaining sheets of dough, make cigar-shaped pastries: cut a sheet of dough lengthwise into 4 equal strips. Take one piece and place it on the work surface with the short end nearest to you. Place 2 teaspoons of filling at one end, fold in the 2 long sides of the dough so they meet in the center over the filling, then roll up the dough to the end, forming a small cigar shape. Moisten the end of the dough with a little water and stick it to the pastry. Repeat this until you use up your filling.

Heat the oil in a large skillet, lower the heat to medium, and fry the triangles and cigar shapes on both sides for about 5 minutes total, or until they're golden brown. Using a slotted spoon, place them on paper towels to drain. Arrange the böreks on a platter. Serve warm or at room temperature with the yogurt-garlic sauce or plain yogurt for dipping.

BREADS AND BÖREKS

~~~~~~~~~~~~~~~~~~~~~~~~~~

THE DAY IN TURKEY STARTS WITH bread, and it ends with bread. Many different types of bread were developed during the Ottoman Empire: loaves, flat breads, griddle breads, stuffed breads and bread rings, called *simit*, that are dipped into molasses and coated with sesame seeds before they are baked.

People in Turkey purchase their bread from the local bakeries, and wonderful aromas permeate the morning air of villages. Some cooks make their own bread, especially the *katmer* (flaky griddle bread), and *lahmacun* (meat-topped flat bread). Lahmacuns are often accompanied by *ayran*, a yogurt drink, or are simply eaten with plain yogurt.

Pita bread has become common all over the world. Its pocket holds any variety of fillings. But in Turkey pita bread is cut into chunks and used as a bed for meat dishes, such as *köfte* and other grilled kebabs. At Sultan's Kitchen, we have fresh-baked pita bread delivered daily from a specialty bakery in Boston because there isn't room to bake it ourselves.

Here are some tips for making good bread. Dust your fingers with flour before you knead dough so it won't stick to your fingers. Knead dough on a cool surface, preferably marble or stone. Always put it in a warm place, away from drafts, to rise. I find that bread bakes best on a pizza stone or tile. To place a loaf in the oven, use a baker's peel to minimize handling of the risen loaf. Sprinkle the peel with flour or cornmeal before placing the loaf on it, then slide the loaf into the oven onto a preheated pizza stone or tile.

Böreks, delightfully tasty savory pastries, are the perfect Turkish snack food. In Turkey, they are offered for breakfast and lunch at shops called *börekçi*. In the summertime, people lunch on böreks in open-air cafés with a glass of Turkish tea or ayran. Usually, these savories are made with *yufka* or *böreklik yufka* (a type of filo dough), and the very thin dough gives them a characteristic golden color and crispiness. The börek recipes here use filo dough—use ready-made dough, or make your own filo using the recipe on page 136.

In Turkish villages, home cooks make large quantities of böreks in trays that don't fit in conventional ovens. Instead, they bring their uncooked trays of böreks to the bakery and have them cooked there for a fee.

Böreks are commonly filled with spinach and feta cheese or with spicy ground meats; they can be rolled into cigar shapes, triangles, or simple rectangles. Even vegetables, legumes, and fish or chicken are used to stuff larger böreks, which are then served as a light lunch with a yogurt-garlic sauce and perhaps a salad of tomatoes, cucumbers, and olives (see Çoban Salatası on page 127).

My mother's spinach and feta cheese böreks (page 54) are the lightest and tastiest that I've tasted. They are so good that a neighbor once came to our house with the ingredients and a baking tray and asked my mother to make them for her. My mother complied with pleasure that first time, but was surprised when other neighbors came to her with the same request!

~~~~~~~~~~~~~~~~~~~~

Katmer

Flaky Griddle Bread

MAKES 12

This classic flat bread can be filled with the meat filling below, with Peynirli, a cheese filling (page 48), or with Ispanakli, a spinach filling (page 54). Serve it with ayran or with a fruit compote (see Dessert, Fruit Compotes, and Drinks).

KIYMALI (MEAT FILLING)

2 tablespoons virgin olive oil
1 small Spanish onion, finely diced (1/2 cup)
3 garlic cloves, minced
3/4 pound ground lean lamb or beef
2 teaspoons paprika
2 teaspoons ground cumin
2 teaspoons Turkish red pepper or ground red pepper
1/4 cup finely chopped fresh Italian parsley
Salt and freshly ground black pepper

5 cups all-purpose, unbleached flour, plus extra
      for dusting
4 eggs
1 teaspoon salt
1/4 cup (1/2 stick) unsalted butter, softened, plus extra,
      melted for brushing
1 1/4 cups water (70° F)
Ayran (page 151) or plain yogurt, to serve

To make the meat filling, heat the olive oil in a medium-size skillet, and cook the onion and garlic for about 2 minutes, until they're softened but not brown. Using a wooden spoon, add the ground lamb or beef, paprika, cumin, Turkish red pepper, and parsley. Season with salt and pepper. Cook the mixture gently for about 5 minutes, stirring well to break up the meat. Remove the skillet from the heat and let the mixture cool.

Sift the flour into a large bowl. Make a well in the center. Add the eggs, salt, butter, and water. Mix well. On a cool, heavily floured work surface (preferably marble), turn out the dough and knead it for about 2 minutes, until it's smooth. Shape the dough into a long cylinder, then cut it into 12 equal pieces with a sharp knife.

On a lightly floured work surface, gently shape each piece into a tight ball. Cover the balls of dough with a damp cloth and let them rest for about 15 minutes. Knead each piece again for about 2 minutes, reshape it into a tight ball, cover it, and let the balls rest again for 15 minutes. Repeat this process one more time.

Sprinkle the balls of dough with flour and flatten each one with the heel of your palm. Roll out each piece into a 12-inch circle. Alternatively, use your hands to stretch the dough by flipping it between your hands back and forth. Spread the filling on each circle. Fold over the dough like an envelope, about 6 inches wide and 8 inches long.

Brush a griddle or large nonstick pan with butter and heat the pan. Cook the katmers one at a time for about 2 minutes, turning them once, until they're lightly browned. Brush the griddle lightly with butter each time before cooking. Serve hot or warm with ayran or plain yogurt.

~ Rustic Turkish Bread (page 46) and Raisin Compote (page 150)

~~~~~~~~~~~~~~~~~

Susamlı ve Çörek
Otlu Pide Ekmeği

**Pita Bread Topped with Sesame and
Black Caraway Seeds**

MAKES 4

I buy the restaurant's pita bread from a local bakery because, unfortunately, I don't have the room to make the quantity that I use every day. It arrives each morning still warm. Homemade pita bread is simple to make, and the sesame seeds and caraway seeds add a fragrant, nutty flavor. This pita bread is much thicker than what you buy in the store. When it comes out of the oven it should be about 1/2 inch thick with a hard crust along the edge.

STARTER
    1 tablespoon active dry or moist fresh yeast (crumbled)
    1 teaspoon sugar
    1 3/4 cups warm water (110°F)

    4 cups unbleached all-purpose flour, divided
    2 teaspoons salt
    3 egg yolks
    1/4 cup milk
    1 1/2 tablespoons sesame seeds
    1 tablespoon black caraway seeds
    Cornmeal, for dusting

In a small bowl, mix together the yeast, sugar, and 1/2 cup of the warm water. Stir and dissolve the yeast well. Let the mixture stand in a warm place for about 10 minutes, until it's frothy.

Sift 1 cup of the flour into a large bowl. Add the yeast mixture and stir well. Cover the bowl with plastic wrap and let it rest in a warm place for 30 minutes, until the mixture has the texture of a sponge. Sift the remaining flour onto this mixture. Add the salt and remaining 1 1/4 cups warm water, and stir well.

Turn out the dough onto a cool, lightly floured work surface (preferably marble), and sprinkle it with flour. Dust your fingers with flour so they won't stick to the dough, and knead the dough for 10 minutes until it's firm and not sticky. Place the dough in a lightly oiled bowl and cover the bowl loosely with plastic wrap or a damp cloth. Let it rest for 1 hour, or until the dough doubles in size.

Heat the oven to 450°F. Place a pizza stone or quarry tile on the middle rack of the oven.

Turn out the risen dough onto a lightly floured work surface. and gently punch out the air and flatten the dough. Form the dough into a cylinder, and then cut it into 4 equal pieces with a sharp knife. Shape each piece into a ball, then press each ball with the heel of your palm to flatten it. Cover the dough balls with a damp cloth and let them rest for 20 minutes.

Use the heel of your palm to flatten each piece of dough some more, and then roll it out into an 8-inch circle, with the outer edge of each round about 1/2 inch thick.

For the glaze, lightly beat together the egg and the milk. Dip your fingertips into the egg glaze and press it firmly all over each round of dough, dipping your fingertips back into the glaze as necessary. Sprinkle each round with the sesame seeds and the caraway seeds.

Sprinkle cornmeal over the pizza stone or onto a baker's peel. Arrange the rounds of dough on the stone and bake the bread in batches for about 10 minutes each batch. The breads will be lightly golden on top when they are done. Serve warm.

NOTE: This dough can be used to make a thinner pita bread with a pocket by rolling it out to 10 inches and baking it as described above. When you take the breads out of the oven, stack them on the counter sideways and upside down, leaning against each other, so they are touching but air flows between them. Cover them with a cloth and let them rest for a few minutes. This allows the bread to soften while the crust stays crispy. To get a pocket, allow the bread to cool completely before cutting it.

~~~~~~~~~~~~~~~~~~

Domates Yahnili ve Kaşar Peynirli Açık Pide

Open-Face Pita Topped with Tomato Ragout and Kasseri Cheese

MAKES 8

This Turkish style "pizza" is seasoned with a wonderfully fragrant spice mixture called *baharat*.

TOMATO RAGOUT

    3 tablespoons virgin olive oil
    1 small Spanish onion, finely diced (1/2 cup)
    4 garlic cloves, minced
    3/4 pound plum tomatoes, peeled,
        seeded and chopped (2 cups)
    1 bay leaf
    1/3 cup tomato juice or water
    Salt and freshly ground black pepper

    Pita bread dough (page 41)
    3/4 pound kasseri cheese, cut into thin slices
    Cornmeal, for dusting
    2 tablespoons finely chopped fresh Italian parsley

BAHARAT

    2 teaspoons dried oregano
    1 teaspoon Turkish red pepper or ground red pepper
    1 tablespoon ground cumin
    Salt and freshly ground black pepper

To prepare the tomato yahni topping, heat the oil in a small saucepan over medium heat and cook the onion, stirring frequently, for about 1 minute, until it's softened but not brown. Add the garlic, tomatoes, bay leaf, and tomato juice. Season with salt and pepper. Bring the mixture to a boil, lower the heat, and simmer for 8 minutes. Discard the bay leaf and set the mixture aside.

Heat the oven to 450°F. Place a pizza stone or quarry tile on the middle rack of the oven.

Dust your fingers with flour so they will not stick to the dough. On a cool, lightly floured work surface (preferably marble), turn out the pita bread dough once it has risen to double its size and gently punch out the air. Roll out the dough into a cylinder and cut it into 8 equal pieces with a sharp knife. Shape each piece into a ball, then press each ball with the heel of your palm to flatten it. Loosely cover the dough balls with plastic wrap or a damp cloth and let them rest for about 20 minutes.

To assemble, flatten each risen piece of dough with the heel of your palm once again. Using a rolling pin, roll out each piece of dough into a 6-inch circle. Divide the tomato ragout among each round of dough, leaving a 1/2-inch border around the edge. Top each piece with 3–4 slices of kasseri cheese.

Sprinkle cornmeal over the pizza stone or on a baker's peel. Bake in batches for about 10 minutes each batch. Meanwhile, mix the ingredients for the baharat, seasoning with salt and pepper. Sprinkle the baharat over the hot bread and garnish with the parsley. Serve hot or warm.

~ *Top to bottom:* Southern-Style Pita Topped with Spicy Lamb (page 44) and an Open-Face Pita Topped with Tomato Ragout and Kasseri Cheese (this page), served with a glass of ayran (page 151)

~~~~~~~~~~~~~~~~~

Zeytinli, Kekikli ve Biberiyeli Ekmek

Olive and Herb Bread

MAKES 2 ROUND LOAVES

This aromatic bread is mostly baked in villages for special occasions.

    1 tablespoon plus two teaspoons active dry or
        moist fresh yeast (crumbled)
    2 teaspoons sugar
    1/2 cup warm water (110°F)
    5 1/2 cups unbleached all-purpose flour, sifted,
        plus extra for dusting
    1 cup whole wheat flour
    1/3 cup extra-virgin olive oil, plus extra for brushing
    1 tablespoon chopped fresh or dry oregano
    1 tablespoon chopped fresh or dry rosemary
    2 cups water (70°F)
    1 tablespoon salt
    1/2 cup pitted oil-cured black olives
    Cornmeal for dusting

In a small bowl, place the yeast, sugar, and 1/2 cup warm water. Stir until the yeast has dissolved. Let the mixture stand in a warm place for about 10 minutes, until it's frothy.

Place the yeast mixture in a large bowl. Add both flours, the olive oil, oregano, rosemary, and 2 cups water and mix well. Dust your hands with flour. Turn out the dough onto a cool, lightly floured surface (preferably marble) and knead it about 7 to 8 minutes. Flatten the dough and sprinkle on the salt. Dust the olives with a little flour and put them on the dough. Fold the dough in half and knead for 2 more minutes, until it's smooth and satiny and springs back when touched. If it's still sticky, add a little more flour and knead it for 1 more minute.

Transfer the dough to a large, lightly oiled bowl and dust it lightly with flour. Cover the bowl loosely with a cloth and let it rest in a warm place that is not drafty (between 80 and 85°F is best) for about 2 to 2 1/2 hours or until the dough doubles in size.

Turn out the risen dough onto a lightly floured work surface and punch out the air. Divide the dough in half. Knead each piece for about 2 to 3 minutes and shape it into a tight oval loaf.

Leave both loaves on the work surface or place them on a floured tray about 4 inches apart. Dust them lightly with flour and cover them loosely with a cloth. Let them rest for 30 to 45 minutes or until they double in size (again the best temperature for this is between 80 and 85°F).

Preheat the oven to 425°F. Place a pizza stone or quarry tile on the middle rack of the oven. To give the bread a nice crust, place 2 cups of boiling water in each of two deep baking pans and place the pans on the bottom of the oven (one on each side) about 20 minutes before you are ready to put your loaves to bake. Or, you can mist some cold water into the oven during the first 10 minutes of baking at five-minute intervals using a spray bottle (about 4 or 5 sprays).

Sprinkle a baker's peel with the cornmeal. Gently place the risen loaves one at a time onto the peel. Using a single-edge razor blade or the tip of a small, very sharp knife, make a few 1/2-inch-deep slashes on top of each loaf.

Gently slide or place the loaves onto the pizza stone and bake for 35 minutes. To check the loaves for doneness, tap the bottoms with your fingertip, and if they don't sound hollow, bake them for 5 more minutes. When done, remove the loaves from the oven and gently brush the tops with olive oil. Set them on a wire rack to cool before slicing.

~~~~~~~~~~~~~~~~~

Lahmacun

Southern-Style Pita Topped with Spicy Lamb

MAKES 8

This flat bread from the southeastern region is very popular all over Turkey. As soon as it comes out of the oven you can brush the edges with melted butter or quickly swipe it with solid butter, but it is also delicious as is. Garnish the breads with lemon wedges and parsley sprigs, and serve with plain yogurt or ayran.

SPICY LAMB TOPPING
    1/2 pound medium-lean lamb, ground twice
    1 small Spanish onion, finely diced (1/2 cup)
    3 plum tomatoes, peeled, seeded and finely diced (1 cup)
    1/2 bunch finely chopped fresh Italian parsley
    3 garlic cloves, minced
    1 tablespoon Turkish red pepper or ground red pepper
    2 teaspoons paprika
    Salt
    1/2 cup cold water

Pita bread dough (page 41)
Cornmeal, for dusting
Butter

To prepare the lamb topping, place all the topping ingredients in a bowl and mix well. Season with salt.

Preheat the oven to 450°F. Place a pizza stone or quarry tile on the middle rack of the oven.

Dust you fingers with flour. On a cool, lightly floured work surface (preferably marble), turn out the pita dough once it has risen to double its size. Gently punch out the air and roll out the dough into a cylinder and cut it into 8 equal pieces with a sharp knife. Shape each piece into a ball, then press each ball with the heel of your palm to flatten it. Loosely cover the dough with plastic wrap or a damp cloth and let them rest in a warm place for about 20 minutes.

To assemble, flatten each piece of dough with the heel of your palm once again. Using a rolling pin, roll out each piece of dough into a 10-inch circle. Divide the spicy lamb mixture among the rounds of dough, spreading it thinly and leaving a 1/2-inch border around the edges.

Sprinkle cornmeal over the pizza stone or on your baker's peel. Bake the lahmacuns in batches for about 7 minutes each batch, until the meat is browned. Remove the breads from the oven and brush the edge of each one with melted butter. Garnish and serve warm or at room temperature.

~~~~~~~~~~~~~~~~~

Nohutlu Köy Ekmeği

Peasant Bread with Chickpeas

MAKES 1 ROUND LOAF (10 INCHES X 2 INCHES)

This bread is my mother's recipe. It is unusual because it contains whole chickpeas. The starter must be made a day in advance.

STARTER
1/2 cup whole dried chickpeas
1 cup warm water (110°F)
2 tablespoons sugar
4 tablespoons unbleached all-purpose wheat flour

DOUGH
3 cups water
5 or 6 dried or fresh bay leaves

4 cups unbleached all-purpose flour, sifted,
    plus extra for dusting
2 1/2 cups barley flour
1 tablespoon plus 2 teaspoons salt
Extra-virgin olive oil for brushing

TOPPING
2 teaspoons fennel seeds
1 tablespoon black caraway seeds
1 tablespoon sesame seeds
2 teaspoons poppy seeds

To make the starter, finely grind half of the chickpeas in a coffee grinder and place them in a bowl. Add the remaining chickpeas, warm water, sugar, and flour. Stir the mixture, cover, and place it in a warm place (70–80°F) overnight.

The next day, mix and reserve the topping mixture.

To make the dough, bring 3 cups of water to a boil, add the bay leaves, and simmer for about 5 minutes. Strain the water and let it cool to room temperature (about 70°F). In a large bowl, mix the flours with the salt, the starter, and the bay leaf–infused water. Dust your fingers with flour. Turn out the dough onto a cool, lightly floured surface (preferably marble), and knead it for about 2 minutes. The dough will be wet and sticky.

Transfer the dough to a lightly oiled bowl and cover it with a cloth or plastic wrap. Let the dough rest in a warm place (between 75 and 80°F) for 4 to 5 hours, or until it bubbles.

Heat the oven to 375°F.

Lightly brush the inside of a 10-inch-diameter x 2-inch high round baking pan with oil. Uncover the dough, which should still be soft and sticky, and put it into the baking pan. Brush the top of the dough with olive oil and make a few cuts on the top with the tip of a very sharp, small knife. Sprinkle on the topping mixture.

To give the bread a nice crust, place 2 cups of boiling water in each of two deep pans and place them on each side of the oven bottom about 20 minutes before you are ready to bake your loaves. Or, you can mist some cold water into the oven at 5-minute intervals during the first 15 minutes of baking using a spray bottle (about 4 or 5 sprays each time). Slide the bread pan onto the middle rack. Bake the bread for 30 to 35 minutes, or until the top is golden brown.

Remove the bread from the pan by inverting it onto the counter. Cover it with a clean cloth and let it rest for a few minutes. Brush the top of the bread with olive oil and serve warm.

Türk Ekmeği

Rustic Turkish Bread

MAKES 2 OVAL LOAVES

In the village where my mother was born they baked this bread using starter made with crushed chickpeas that was over a hundred years old.

SOURDOUGH STARTER
  1½ cups unbleached all-purpose flour, sifted
  ¾ cup lukewarm water (75 to 80°F)

DOUGH
  1 tablespoon plus two teaspoons active dry or moist fresh yeast (crumbled)
  1 tablespoon sugar
  ½ cup warm water (110°F)
  6 cups unbleached all-purpose flour, sifted, plus extra for dusting
  2 cups lukewarm water (70°F), divided
  1 tablespoon salt
  Cornmeal for dusting

To make the starter, place ½ cup of the flour and ¼ cup lukewarm water in a container. Stir the mixture well, cover, and let it sit at room temperature (between 70 and 75°F) overnight.

The next day, add ½ cup of the flour and ¼ cup of the water to the container, mix well, cover, and let it sit at room temperature overnight. Repeat one more time.

On the fourth day, the starter is ready to use. It can be stored in the refrigerator for up to 4 days. When you are ready to make the bread, let it sit at room temperature at least 2 hours before you need it.

To make the bread, place the yeast, sugar, and ½ cup warm water in a small bowl. Stir until the yeast has dissolved and let it stand in a warm place for about 10 minutes, until it's frothy.

Place the yeast mixture into a large bowl, stir in the flour and the sourdough starter in small pieces. Add the 2 cups of lukewarm water and mix well.

Dust your fingers with flour. Place the dough on a cool, lightly floured surface (preferably marble), and knead it about 7 to 8 minutes. Flatten out the dough and sprinkle on the salt. Fold the dough in half and knead for 2 more minutes, until it is smooth and satiny and springs back when touched. If it is still sticky, add a little more flour and knead for one more minute.

Place the dough on a lightly floured work surface. Sprinkle a little flour over the dough, cover it with a cloth, and let it rest in a warm place (about 80 to 85°F) for 2 to 2½ hours, until it doubles in size.

Put the dough back onto a lightly floured work surface and punch out the air. Divide the dough in half and knead each piece for 2 to 3 minutes. Shape each piece into a tight oval loaf.

Sprinkle flour on the loaves, cover with a cloth, and let them rest in a warm place 4 inches apart for 30 to 45 minutes, or until they double in size.

Preheat the oven to 425°F and place a pizza stone or quarry tile on the middle rack of the oven. To give the bread a nice crust, place 2 cups of boiling water in each of two deep baking pans and place them on each side of the the oven bottom about 20 minutes before baking the loaves. Or, you can mist some cold water into the oven during the first 15 minutes of baking at five-minute intervals using a spray bottle (about 4 or 5 sprays each time).

Sprinkle a baker's peel with cornmeal. Gently place the risen loaves one at a time onto the peel. Using a single-edge razor blade or the tip of a small, very sharp knife, make a few ½-inch-deep slashes on top of each loaf. Gently slide or place the loaves onto the pizza stone and bake for 40 minutes.

To check the loaves for doneness, tap the bottoms with your fingertip and if they don't sound hollow, bake them for 5 more minutes. When done, remove the loaves from the oven and set them on a wire rack to cool before slicing.

~ *Clockwise from top:* Olive and Herb Bread (page 44), Pita Bread Topped with Sesame and Black Caraway Seeds (page 41) and Flaky Griddle Bread (page 40)

Çerkez Puf Böreği
Circassian Böreks
MAKES 30 PASTRIES

This börek is made with the cheese filling (Peynirli) below or with the meat filling (Kiymali) on page 40.

PEYNIRLI (CHEESE FILLING)
    12 ounces crumbled feta cheese (1 1/2 cups)
    1 egg
    1/2 cup finely chopped fresh dill

    3 1/2 cups unbleached all-purpose flour,
        plus extra for dusting
    1 tablespoon salt
    3 egg yolks, lightly beaten
    1/2 cup plain yogurt
    1/2 cup milk
    1 tablespoon lemon juice
    6 tablespoons unsalted clarified butter (page 7)
    1 1/2 cups light olive oil or vegetable oil

To make the cheese filling, mix the cheese, egg, and dill in a bowl and set the mixture aside.

To make the dough, sift the flour and salt onto a work surface—preferably cold marble or wood—or sift them into a large bowl. Make a well in the center and add the egg yolks, yogurt, milk, and lemon juice. Gradually work the ingredients into the flour to form a firm ball of dough. Place the dough on a lightly floured work surface and knead it well for about 5 minutes or until it's smooth and satiny. Shape the dough into a tight ball. Cover it with a damp cloth and let it rest for about 20 minutes.

Place the dough on a lightly floured work surface and sprinkle a little flour over the dough. Roll out the dough into a thin circle about 18 inches in diameter. Spread the melted butter over the dough.

Using a sharp knife, cut the dough from the edge toward the center into 8 wedge-shaped slices about 5 inches long, leaving an 8-inch diameter circle in the center of the dough. Fold each slice toward the center and on top of each other. Cover the dough with a damp cloth and let it rest for 30 minutes.

Lightly sprinkle flour over the

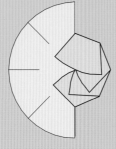

work surface and over the dough to prevent the dough from sticking. Roll out the dough to a circle about 22 inches in diameter—it should be very thinly rolled out. Using a 4-inch pastry cutter, cut out 30 circles of dough. Spoon a little of the cheese or meat filling in the center of the pastry circles. Fold the dough in half to enclose the filling, forming half-moon shapes. Seal the edges securely by pressing them gently with a fork.

Heat the olive oil in a deep pan for frying. It is important that the oil be hot enough (about 350–365°F) so the böreks do not become greasy. To test the hot oil, dip the corner of one börek into the oil, taking care not to burn yourself. If the oil sizzles on contact with the dough, it's ready. Gently fry each pastry until it's puffed and golden brown, about 4 minutes each. Drain the böreks on paper towels. Serve hot.

Mercimekli Ispanaklı Bükme Böreği
Lentil and Spinach Böreks
MAKES 9 BÖREKS

This recipe is from the Aegean and Mediterranean regions of Turkey.

    4 cups unbleached all-purpose flour,
        plus extra for dusting
    1/2 teaspoon salt
    2 eggs, lightly beaten
    1 tablespoon white wine vinegar
    1 cup chilled water

FILLING
    2 tablespoons virgin olive oil
    1 bunch scallions, finely chopped, white parts only
        (1/2 cup)
    6 ounces fresh spinach, trimmed and finely chopped
        (1 cup)
    2 small tomatoes, peeled, seeded, and chopped
    3/4 cup cooked green lentils
    Salt and freshly ground black pepper

    3/4 pound (3 sticks) unsalted butter, chilled

GLAZE
    1 egg yolk
    2 tablespoons milk

To make the dough, sift the flour and salt onto a work surface—preferably cold marble or wood—or sift them into a large
bowl. Make a well in the center and add the eggs, vinegar, and water. Gradually work the ingredients into the flour to make a firm
ball of dough. Place the dough on a lightly floured work surface
and knead it for about 8 minutes, or until it's smooth. Shape the
dough into a round and score it with a sharp knife. Wrap the
dough securely in plastic wrap and refrigerate it for at least 1 hour.

Heat the oven to 350°F.

To make the filling, heat the oil in a skillet over medium heat,
and gently cook the scallions for 1 minute. Stir in the spinach and
tomatoes and cook for 2 minutes. Remove the mixture from the
heat and stir in the lentils. Season with salt and pepper. Let the
filling cool.

~ *From top to bottom:* Circassian Börek and two Lentil and
Spinach Böreks

On a lightly floured work surface, roll out the chilled dough to
an 18-inch square. Wrap the butter in a damp cloth. Using a rolling
pin, pound the butter and roll it out to form a 6-inch square.

Place the square of butter in the center of the dough and fold
the dough in half over the butter. Roll out the dough again to
make an 18-inch square. Sprinkle the work surface and dough from
time to time with flour to prevent the dough from sticking. Cut the
dough into 12 rectangles.

Divide the filling into 12 portions. Place one portion of the
lentil-and-spinach filling in the center of each piece of dough. Make
an envelope out of each rectangle by folding the top and bottom
edges in toward the middle and gently pressing the edges with your
fingertips to seal the fold.

Line a baking pan with parchment paper and place each pastry, folded side up, on the pan. Mix the egg yolk and milk for the
glaze. Brush the glaze on top of each pastry. Bake the böreks for
about 30 minutes, or until they're golden brown. Serve warm.

~~~~~~~~~~~~~~

Mantı

Ground Lamb–Filled Dumplings with Yogurt-Garlic Sauce

SERVES 6

These tiny dumplings are the specialty of eastern and southern Turkey. The are time-consuming to prepare but very good.

To roll out the dough, you will need a 3/4-inch diameter, 30-inch long rolling pin (*oklava*). A wooden dowel from the hardware store works well.

    2 cups unbleached all-purpose flour,
        plus extra for dusting
    1 teaspoon salt
    2 eggs, lightly beaten
    1 tablespoon virgin olive oil
    1/2 cup cold milk

    2 cups lamb stock (page 58) or
        chicken stock (page 58)
    1 recipe Yogurt-Garlic Sauce (page 13)

FILLING
    1/2 pound ground lean lamb or beef
    1 small Spanish onion, grated (1/2 cup)
    1/4 cup finely chopped fresh Italian parsley
    Salt and freshly ground black pepper

TOPPING
    5 1/3 tablespoons unsalted clarified butter
        (page 7)
    1 teaspoon paprika
    1/2 teaspoon Turkish red pepper or
        ground red pepper
    1 teaspoon dried mint

Sift the flour and salt into a large bowl. Make a well in the center and add the eggs, oil, and milk, mixing well. Turn out the mixture onto a lightly floured work surface and gently knead it for about 8 minutes, dusting the dough and your hands from time to time to prevent the dough from sticking. Cover the dough with a damp cloth and let it rest for 45 minutes.

To prepare the filling. Combine the lamb, onion, and parsley in a small bowl. Season with salt and pepper. Cover the bowl and refrigerate.

Heat the oven to 375°F.

Turn out the rested dough onto a lightly floured work surface. Using an oklava, roll out a very thin— about 1/16 inch thick—22-inch circle. Dust the work surface lightly with flour occasionally to help prevent the dough from sticking. Cut the dough into 2-inch-wide strips, then cut 2-inch strips, crosswise, to make 80 2-inch squares. Discard the irregular pieces.

Place about 1/2 teaspoon of the filling onto each square. Bring all four corners of each square together and twist them with your fingertips to close tightly. Gently press each dumpling to flatten it slightly. While working, dust your fingertips with flour from time to time.

Place the dumplings onto a lightly greased 2-inch-deep baking pan. Bake them for about 15 minutes, until they're lightly browned. Remove the pan from the oven and pour over the stock. Return the pan to the oven, lower the heat to 325°F, and bake for another 10 minutes.

In a small saucepan, heat the butter for the topping and stir in the paprika, Turkish pepper, and mint.

Using a slotted spoon, transfer the dumplings onto warmed serving plates. Pour over the yogurt-garlic sauce and drizzle a little of the herb topping over each serving.

~ *From top to bottom:* Ground Lamb–Filled Dumplings with Yogurt-Garlic Sauce and Börek with Swiss Chard and Walnuts (page 52) served with Turkish tea (page 150)

~~~~~~~~~~~~~~~~~

Pazılı ve Cevizli Kol Böreği

Böreks with Swiss Chard and Walnuts

MAKES 8 BÖREKS

1½ pounds Swiss chard, coarsely chopped
6 tablespoons virgin olive oil, divided
½ cup unsalted clarified butter (page 7), divided
½ cup coarsely chopped walnuts
⅓ cup finely chopped scallions (white parts only)
2 eggs, divided
6 ounces crumbled feta cheese (¾ cup)
1 teaspoon Turkish red pepper or ground red pepper
Salt and freshly ground black pepper
¼ cup milk
1 pound filo dough, about 20 to 22 sheets

GLAZE
2 egg yolks
2 tablespoons milk

Cook the chopped Swiss chard in 2 cups water until it's wilted. Drain the Swiss chard well and squeeze out the excess liquid.

In a large skillet, heat 3 tablespoons of the olive oil and 3 tablespoons of the clarified butter over medium heat. Add the walnuts and scallions and cook for 1 minute, stirring. Add the Swiss chard and continue cooking for 2 minutes, stirring with a wooden spoon. Remove the skillet from the heat and let the mixture cool. Add 1 egg, the feta cheese, and Turkish red pepper. Season with salt and pepper. Mix well and set the mixture aside.

Heat the oven to 350°F.

Warm up the remaining clarified butter and mix it well in a bowl with the milk, the other egg, and the remaining olive oil. Brush a little of this mixture onto the surface of a 13 x 18 x 1-inch baking pan. Unroll the filo dough and place 1 sheet on a work surface. Brush it lightly with the butter mixture. Layer all of the filo sheets in the package, one at a time, brushing each lightly with the butter mixture.

Spread all of the Swiss chard filling over the dough evenly. Loosely roll up the dough over the filling, tucking in both ends. Transfer the roll to the baking pan, seam side down. Mix the egg yolks and milk and brush this egg wash all over the roll of pastry.

Bake the roll for about 35 minutes, or until it's golden brown. Let it stand for 10 minutes, then cut off about an inch of pastry from each end. Cut the remaining roll into eight 2-inch slices and serve.

~~~~~~~~~~~~~~~~~

Su Böreği

Water Böreks

MAKES 12 LARGE OR 24 SMALL BÖREKS

This is truly the king of the böreks, and although it is very time-consuming to prepare, it is delicious and much lighter than other böreks. As a child in Turkey, I would buy these from *börekçi* and eat them with a glass of milk for breakfast.

I have provided two different filling recipes. You will need an oklava or a ¾-inch-diameter, 30-inch long wooden dowel to prepare this recipe. Instead of making the dough yourself, you can buy *yufka* from mail-order suppliers.

CHEESE FILLING
1 bunch scallions, chopped, white part only (½ cup)
12 ounces crumbled feta cheese (1½ cups)
¼ cup coarsely chopped fresh Italian parsley leaves
2 eggs
½ cup milk

MEAT FILLING
2 tablespoons virgin olive oil
1 small Spanish onion, diced (½ cup)
3 garlic cloves, minced
2 pounds ground lean lamb or beef
2 medium tomatoes, peeled, and chopped (1 cup)
¾ cup coarsely chopped fresh Italian parsley leaves
Salt and freshly ground black pepper to taste

DOUGH
3½ cups unbleached all-purpose flour, sifted
1 tablespoon plus 1 teaspoon salt
5 eggs, room temperature
½ cup water, room temperature (about 70°F)
½ cup cornstarch

10 cups ice cubes
1¼ cups unsalted clarified butter (page 7)

GLAZE
2 egg yolks
¼ cup milk

Prepare whichever filling mixture you prefer. For the cheese filling, mix all the ingredients in a bowl and set it aside.

For the meat filling, heat the olive oil over medium heat in a heavy-bottomed pan and cook the onion until it is softened but not browned. Add the garlic, meat, tomatoes, parsley, salt, and pepper, and stir well. Lower the heat and cook the mixture until almost all the liquid has been absorbed, about 15 minutes. Set the pan aside and let the filling cool.

To make the dough, sift the flour with the salt onto a work table, preferably one with a wooden top. Make a well in the center for the eggs and water. Add the eggs and the water and mix the ingredients slowly to make a dough. Knead the dough, dusting it and your hands with cornstarch now and then to prevent the dough from sticking, until it is smooth and satiny looking, about 4 minutes.

Cover the dough with a damp cloth and let it rest at room temperature for about 30 minutes.

Knead the dough again for about 4 minutes, cover it with a damp cloth, and let it rest for about another 30 minutes.

Sprinkle the work surface and the dough lightly with cornstarch. Roll out the dough into a rectangle about 24 inches long and cut it into 16 equal pieces.

Gently flatten each piece of dough by pressing it with the heel of your palm. Sprinkle the pieces lightly with cornstarch and spread them out so they don't touch one another other. Cover the pieces with a damp cloth and let them rest for about 15 minutes.

With a rolling pin, roll out each piece of dough into a 12-inch-diameter circle, lightly dusting both sides with cornstarch. Stack the pieces into 2 piles of 8 each and cover them with a damp cloth.

Using an oklava (or a 3/4-inch-diameter, 30-inch-long wooden dowel) roll out each piece of dough again, one at a time, by pressing down on the center of the dough with the oklava and pushing it toward the outer edge of the dough and then pulling the oklava back toward you, rotating the dough with a quick motion after every few rolls. Each piece of dough should be rolled as thin as possible into a 14 x 20-inch oval.

Sprinkle the pieces lightly with cornstarch, place them in a stack on top of one another and cover them with a damp cloth.

Heat the oven to 350°F.

In a large, deep baking pan, slightly larger than the size of the dough, add 8 cups of cold water and a dash of salt. Bring the water to a boil and lower the heat. Place the ice cubes and 6 cups water in another deep pan that is also slightly larger than the size of the dough, and place it next to the stove. You will plunge the cooked börek dough into this cold water to stop it from cooking. Also position a large colander upside down near the ice-water-filled pan and cover it with a cloth—you will drape the cooked dough over it to dry.

Brush the inside of a 12 x 18 x 3-inch baking pan with clarified butter and set it aside.

Take one piece of dough and drop it into the hot water. Using a slotted spoon, gently push the dough around in the water for 25 to 30 seconds. Carefully scoop out the dough with one or two slotted spoons and drop it into the ice water, leaving it there for 10 to 15 seconds. Lift the dough out of the ice water, place it on top of the colander, and pat it dry with a dishcloth. Place the dough into the baking tray and brush it with butter.

Repeat this process, quickly cooking 8 pieces of the dough. If the ice cubes melt quickly, add more and drain off some of the water. Spread the filling evenly over the dough in the baking pan.

Continue the boiling, cooling, and drying process with the other 8 pieces of dough, placing each one on top of the filling and brushing it with butter, until you have used up all the dough pieces.

In a small bowl, mix the egg yolks and milk together. Glaze the surface of the dough with the egg yolks and milk and cut the dough into either 12 or 24 pieces, depending on how large you want the böreks. Bake them for 45 to 50 minutes or until the surface is a golden brown. Let them sit at room temperature for about 10 minutes, recut them, and serve warm.

NOTE: If the dough splits when you are working with it, just patch it.

~~~~~~~~~~~~~~~~~~

Ispanaklı Peynirli Tepsi Böreği

Spinach and Feta Cheese Böreks

MAKES 12 LARGE OR 24 BÖREKS

ISPANAKLI (SPINACH FILLING)

3 pounds fresh spinach, trimmed
1/4 cup virgin olive oil
1/4 cup unsalted clarified butter (page 7)
1 bunch scallions, trimmed and finely chopped
    (include white parts only) (1/2 cup)
2 eggs
12 ounces crumbled feta cheese (1 1/2 cups)
1/3 cup finely chopped fresh Italian parsley
Salt and freshly ground black pepper

PASTRY

1/4 cup unsalted clarified butter (page 7)
1/3 cup milk
1/4 cup virgin olive oil
1 egg
1 pound filo dough, about 20 to 22 sheets

GLAZE

2 egg yolks
1/4 cup milk

Heat the oven to 375°F.

To make the filling, cook the spinach in 1 cup boiling water over medium heat, stirring often, until it's wilted. Drain the spinach well and squeeze it dry; then chop it. In a large skillet over medium heat, heat the olive oil and the clarified butter. Stir in the scallions and spinach and cook for 2 minutes. Let the mixture cool. Add the eggs, feta cheese, and parsley to the cooled spinach mixture. Season with salt and pepper. Set the mixture aside.

To prepare the pastry, place the butter in a bowl along with the milk, olive oil, and egg and mix them together. Brush this mixture on a 13 x 18 x 1-inch baking pan. Carefully unroll the filo dough and place 1 sheet on the pan. Lightly brush the dough with a little of the butter mixture. Place a second piece of dough over the first and brush it with the butter mixture. Continue layering in this manner until there are 10 layers of filo dough. Put a damp towel on the remaining filo dough to keep it from drying out.

Spread all of the spinach mixture evenly over the filo dough in the pan. Cover the mixture with another sheet of dough, brush the dough with the butter mixture, and continue layering and brushing each layer with butter until all the filo dough is used. Make the glaze by combining the egg yolks with the milk. Brush this glaze over the top. Using a sharp knife, cut the pastry into 12 squares or 24 triangles. Bake for 20 minutes, then lower the heat to 325°F and bake for another 20 minutes. When they're ready, the top will be light brown and crispy. Let the böreks stand for 10 minutes before serving.

~ *Top to bottom:* Water Börek (page 52) and Spinach and Feta Cheese Böreks served with a glass of ayran (page 151)

SOUPS

~ ~

MANY TURKISH MEALS, including early-morning breakfasts and late-night snacks, start with soup. So popular are soups in Turkey that *çorbacı* restaurants serve nothing but that, and some even specialize in a particular kind of soup. Restaurants that serve tripe soup are open very late because this soup is thought to cure hangovers. Lemon juice and vinegar are often added to soups to give them a bright tanginess. As with all Turkish foods, some soups are served mostly in warm months and some in cold months. A delicately flavored white soup made with yogurt and mint or a bright red, ripe tomato soup is perfect for a warm summer evening. A hearty, thick broth with beans, fresh vegetables, and a bit of lamb or chicken added for flavoring or a colorful mackerel soup is an entire meal in itself for a winter lunch or supper.

I have many favorite soups: the one made with *tarhana* (page 70), an intensely flavored dried dough that takes up to two weeks to make, and the anchovy soup on page 64, which uses the fresh anchovies (*hamsi*) that are so popular in the Black Sea region of Turkey. The recipe here is from my uncle who used to make it for me when I was a child.

~~~~~~~~~~~~~~~~

Tavuk Suyu

Chicken Stock

MAKES 2 QUARTS

3 pounds chicken carcass with some meat
    still on the bones
1 small Spanish onion, coarsely chopped (^{1}/2 cup)
2 celery ribs, coarsely chopped
2 leeks, trimmed and coarsely chopped
    (include white parts only)
2 carrots, coarsely chopped (^{3}/4 cup)
2 garlic cloves, crushed
1 dried or fresh bay leaf
2 whole cloves
6 black peppercorns, slightly crushed
4 sprigs fresh Italian parsley

Place the chicken bones in a large pot. Add 2 quarts cold water, the vegetables, garlic, bay leaf, cloves, peppercorns, and the parsley. Cover the pot and bring the liquid to a boil. Lower the heat to maintain a steady boil and cook for about 1 hour. Carefully skim off any foam and fat that rise to the surface. Add extra water if needed to keep the bones and vegetables covered.

Strain the stock through a double thickness of cheesecloth or through a fine sieve into a large bowl. Discard the vegetables and bones. Let the stock cool, uncovered. Cover and refrigerate or freeze the stock until you're ready to use it. Before using the stock, skim off and discard the hardened layer of fat. Chicken stock keeps for up to one week in the refrigerator.

~~~~~~~~~~~~~~~~

Et Suyu

Lamb Stock

MAKES 2 QUARTS

3 pounds lamb shank bones with some meat on them
1 medium Spanish onion, coarsely chopped (^{3}/4 cup)
2 celery ribs, coarsely chopped
2 leeks, trimmed and coarsely chopped
    (include white parts only)
2 carrots, coarsely chopped (^{3}/4 cup)
2 garlic cloves, crushed
1 dried or fresh bay leaf
1 sprig fresh thyme
4 sprigs fresh Italian parsley
6 black peppercorns, slightly crushed

Heat the oven to 475°F.

In a roasting pan, spread out the lamb shank bones in a single layer. Roast until well browned all over, turning them a few times, about 1 hour.

Drain off any excess fat and transfer the lamb to a deep pot. Add 2^1/2 quarts cold water and all the remaining ingredients. Bring the liquid to a boil, then lower the heat, cover the pot, and gently boil for about 4 hours. Carefully skim off any foam and fat that rise to the surface. Add extra water if needed to keep the bones and vegetables covered.

Strain the stock through a double thickness of cheesecloth or through a fine sieve into a large bowl. Let the stock cool, uncovered. Cover the bowl and refrigerate. Before using or freezing the stock, discard the hardened layer of fat that rises to the surface of the stock. Lamb stock keeps for up to one week in the refrigerator.

~ *Left to right:* Egg, Lemon, Chicken, and Rice Soup (page 63) and High Plateau Soup (page 60)

Balık Suyu

Fish Stock

MAKES 2 QUARTS

3 pounds fish bones, trimmings and some
    flesh included
1 small Spanish onion, coarsely chopped (1/2 cup)
2 celery ribs, coarsely chopped
2 leeks, trimmed and coarsely chopped
    (include white parts only)
2 carrots, coarsely chopped (3/4 cup)
2 garlic cloves, crushed
1 dried or fresh bay leaf
1 sprig fresh thyme
4 sprigs fresh parsley
6 black peppercorns, slightly crushed
1 tablespoon salt

Wash the fish bones under cold running water. Place them in a deep pot with 2 quarts cold water and all the remaining ingredients. Bring the liquid to a boil, then lower the heat, cover the pot, and simmer gently for about 1 hour. Carefully skim off any foam that rises to the surface. Add extra water if needed to keep the bones and vegetables covered.

Strain the stock through a double thickness of cheesecloth or through a fine sieve into a large bowl. Let the stock cool, uncovered. Cover the bowl and refrigerate. Before use or freezing, discard the jellied layer on the surface. Fish stock keeps for up to one week in the refrigerator.

Yayla Çorbası

High Plateau Soup

SERVES 4–6

In Turkish cuisine, there are many different kinds of yogurt soups, with a wide variety of grains and herbs. Most of them come from Anatolia and eastern Turkey, but they are popular everywhere. This wonderfully smooth soup is flavored with mint. The flour and egg yolks stabilize the yogurt and keep it from curdling.

5 cups chicken stock (page 58) or water
1 cup long-grain white rice
2 tablespoons unsalted clarified butter (page 7)
2 cups plain yogurt
2 tablespoons all-purpose flour
3 egg yolks
2 tablespoons dried mint
Salt

TOPPING
2 tablespoons unsalted butter
1 tablespoon paprika
1 tablespoon dried mint

Place the stock, rice, and butter in a heavy medium-size saucepan. Bring the liquid to a boil, then lower the heat to medium, and simmer for about 30 minutes, or until the rice is tender.

Mix the yogurt, flour, and egg yolks until smooth. Stir the mixture into the soup. Add the mint and season with salt. Simmer for another 10 minutes, or until the soup has a creamy consistency.

To make the topping, melt the butter in a small saucepan over low heat; add the paprika and mint, and stir the mixture until it sizzles. Ladle the soup into individual bowls and drizzle the butter mixture over each serving. Serve at once.

~~~~~~~~~~~~~~~~

Ispanaklı Yoğurt Çorbası

Spinach and Yogurt Soup

SERVES 4–6

This spinach yogurt soup is quick and simple to prepare. With its beautiful light green color, it is perfect for serving on a summer day.

1 pound fresh spinach leaves, trimmed
5 cups chicken stock (page 58) or water
2 tablespoons unsalted clarified butter (page 7)
1 small Spanish onion, grated (1/2 cup)
Salt and freshly ground black pepper
2 cups plain yogurt
2 tablespoons all-purpose flour
3 egg yolks
1 1/2 tablespoons lemon juice

TOPPING
2 tablespoons unsalted butter
1 tablespoon paprika

Place the spinach and stock in a large saucepan. Bring the liquid to a boil, then turn off the heat. Using a slotted spoon or skimmer, lift out the spinach leaves. Finely chop the spinach and set it aside. Reserve the stock.

In a heavy medium-size saucepan, heat the butter over medium heat, add the onion, and cook gently for about 2 minutes, until it's softened but not brown. Stir in the chopped spinach. Add the reserved stock and season with salt and pepper. Cover the saucepan and cook for about 15 minutes.

Meanwhile, mix the yogurt, flour, egg yolks, and lemon juice. Hold a sieve over the soup and pour the yogurt mixture into it. Using a wooden spoon or ladle, push the mixture through the sieve, into the soup. Stir the soup, lower the heat, and cook very gently without boiling for another 10 minutes.

To make the topping, melt the butter in a small saucepan over low heat and stir in the paprika. Heat the mixture until it sizzles. Ladle the soup into individual bowls and drizzle the butter mixture over each serving. Serve at once.

~~~~~~~~~~~~~~~~

Naneli Kuru Bezelye Çorbası

Mint Split Pea Soup

SERVES 4–6

This soup has a velvety smooth consistency. The mint and split peas make a good combination.

1 tablespoon virgin olive oil
1 tablespoon unsalted clarified butter (page 7)
1 small Spanish onion, grated (1/2 cup)
1 1/2 cups split peas, soaked overnight and drained (page 7)
6 cups chicken stock (page 58) or water
1/4 cup cornstarch
1 tablespoon dried mint
Salt and freshly ground white pepper
2 tablespoons heavy cream
Plain croutons, for serving (optional)

In a heavy medium-size saucepan, heat the olive oil and the butter together over medium heat. Add the onion and cook for about 2 minutes, or until it's softened but not brown. Stir in the split peas, then add the stock. Cover the saucepan and bring the liquid to a boil; then lower the heat and simmer for about 30 minutes, stirring occasionally, until the peas are cooked and have blended with the stock.

Transfer the hot liquid to a blender or food processor fitted with a metal blade. Process the mixture until it's smooth. Return the soup to the rinsed-out saucepan and keep it hot.

Mix the cornstarch and 1/4 cup cold water. Stir this thickening agent into the hot soup and bring it to a boil, stirring constantly. Lower the heat, add the dried mint, and season with salt and white pepper. Simmer for another 10 minutes. Remove the saucepan from the heat and stir in the cream. Serve at once with croutons, if so desired.

~~~~~~~~~~~~~~~~

Köylü Çorbası

Peasant Soup

SERVES 4–6

This hearty winter soup makes a meal. A squeeze of lemon juice adds a tangy note to the rich flavors.

1/4 cup unsalted clarified butter (page 7)
1 small Spanish onion, finely diced (1/2 cup)
2 garlic cloves, minced
3/4 pound boneless and skinless chicken breast, diced
2 carrots, finely diced (3/4 cup)
2 parsnips, finely diced (3/4 cup)
2 small potatoes, finely diced (3/4 cup)
1 small celeriac knob, peeled and finely diced (3/4 cup)
2 leeks, trimmed and finely sliced (white parts only)
 (3/4 cup)
1 small turnip, finely diced (1/2 cup)
1/4 cup finely chopped fresh Italian parsley
1/4 cup all-purpose flour
6 cups chicken stock (page 58)
Salt and freshly ground black pepper
Lemon wedges

Melt the butter in a heavy medium-size saucepan. Add the onion and garlic and cook gently over medium heat for about 2 minutes, stirring frequently with a wooden spoon, until they're softened but not brown. Add the diced chicken, carrots, parsnips, potatoes, celeriac, leeks, turnips, and parsley. Stir in the flour and mix well until the vegetables and chicken are coated with the flour. Pour in the stock and bring to a boil; then lower the heat, cover the saucepan, and simmer for about 30 minutes, or until all the vegetables are tender. Season with salt and pepper and simmer for another 5 minutes.

Ladle the soup into individual serving bowls. Serve at once with lemon wedges for squeezing over the soup.

~ Peasant Soup

~~~~~~~~~~~~~~~~

Terbiyeli Pirinçli Tavuk Çorbası

Egg, Lemon, Chicken, and Rice Soup

SERVES 4–6

My customers tell me this soup is an excellent cure for colds. It is a rich, creamy combination of chicken soup and lemon juice.

6 cups chicken stock (page 58)
1 1/2 cups long-grain white rice
2 tablespoons unsalted clarified butter (page 7)
1 pound boneless, skinless chicken breast, diced
4 egg yolks
5 tablespoons lemon juice
Salt

Place the stock, rice, and butter in a heavy medium-size saucepan. Bring the liquid to a boil, then lower the heat to medium, cover the saucepan, and simmer for about 30 minutes, or until the rice is tender. Add the diced chicken. Thoroughly blend the egg yolks and lemon juice in a bowl. Gently ladle 1 cup of the hot liquid soup into the bowl and blend well. Then slowly stir this egg mixture into the saucepan. Cook the soup very gently for 5 minutes. Season with salt. Cook over very low heat for about 5 minutes. Do not allow the soup to boil, or it may curdle. Serve at once.

~~~~~~~~~~~~~~~~

Şehriyeli Tavuk Çorbası

Chicken and Vermicelli Soup

SERVES 4–6

3 tablespoons unsalted clarified butter (page 7)
2 tablespoons finely grated Spanish onion
1/2 pound boneless, skinless chicken breast, diced
1 cup vermicelli, broken into 1- to 1 1/2-inch pieces
1 1/2 quarts chicken stock (page 58)
Salt
5 tablespoons lemon juice

In a heavy medium-size pot, melt the butter over medium heat and cook the onion for 1 minute, stirring, until it's softened but not brown. Add the chicken and vermicelli, stirring, for 2 minutes. Add the stock and salt to taste. Bring to a boil, then simmer for about 20 minutes. Add the lemon juice and serve.

~~~~~~~~~~~~~~~~

Hamsi Çorbası

Fresh Anchovy Soup

SERVES 4–6

1½ pound fresh anchovy or small sardine fillets
Salt
6 cups fish stock (page 60) or water
½ cup orzo
2 tablespoons unsalted clarified butter (page 7)
4 egg yolks
5 tablespoons lemon juice
2 tablespoons fresh Italian parsley, finely chopped
Lemon wedges

Wash the fish fillets in cold water. Sprinkle them lightly with salt and put them in a colander to drain. Let them stand about 20 minutes.

Place the fish stock, orzo, and butter in a saucepan and bring to a boil over high heat. Lower the heat to medium, cover, and simmer for about 20 minutes or until the orzo is tender.

Rinse the fish under cold water and add it to the saucepan.

In a bowl, whisk the egg yolks with the lemon juice. Slowly add 1 cup of the hot stock to the egg lemon mixture and blend, then slowly pour the egg mixture into the saucepan. Stir gently and salt to taste. Lower the heat and simmer the soup uncovered for about 10 minutes. Don't let the soup boil or it may curdle.

Serve the soup hot, sprinkled with chopped parsley and garnished with a lemon wedge.

~~~~~~~~~~~~~~~~

Sebzeli Kuru Fasülye Çorbası

White Bean and Vegetable Soup

SERVES 4–6

White beans appear in every kind of Turkish dish. This hearty soup is white with colorful flecks of red and green.

2 tablespoons virgin olive oil
2 tablespoons unsalted clarified butter (page 7)
1 small Spanish onion, finely diced (½ cup)
2 garlic cloves, minced
2 large tomatoes, peeled, seeded, and finely
    chopped (1½ cups)
2 tablespoons tomato paste
1½ cups great northern beans or small lima beans,
    soaked and drained (page 7)
1½ quarts chicken stock (page 58) or water
1 carrot, finely diced (½ cup)
1 celery rib, diced (½ cup)
½ teaspoon Turkish red pepper or ground red pepper
¼ cup cornstarch
Salt and freshly ground black pepper
¼ cup finely chopped fresh Italian parsley

In a heavy medium-size saucepan, heat the oil and the butter together over medium heat. Add the onion and garlic and cook gently for about 2 minutes, stirring, until they're softened but not brown. Add the chopped tomatoes, tomato paste, beans, and stock. Bring the soup to a boil; then lower the heat and simmer for about 30 minutes. Add the carrot, celery, and Turkish pepper and cook for another 30 minutes, stirring frequently, until the beans are cooked.

In a small bowl, mix the cornstarch and ½ cup cold water to make a smooth paste. Stir this thickening agent into the hot soup. Season with salt and pepper. Bring the soup to a boil; then lower the heat, cover the saucepan, and simmer for another 10 minutes.

Ladle the soup into individual bowls, sprinkle with chopped parsley, and serve.

~ Fish and Vegetable Soup (page 66)

~~~~~~~~~~~~~~~~

Sebzeli Uskumru Çorbası

Fish and Vegetable Soup

SERVES 4–6

2 to 2½ pounds whole mackerel, skinned, filleted,
  and cut into 2-inch chunks
1½ quarts fish stock (page 60) or water
4 tablespoons virgin olive oil
1 small Spanish onion, finely diced (½ cup)
4 garlic cloves, minced
2 small potatoes, diced (¾ cup)
2 carrots, diced (¾ cup)
2 celery ribs, diced (1 cup)
3 tomatoes, skinned, seeded, and finely diced (2 cups)
1 tablespoon finely chopped fresh Italian parsley
1 tablespoon finely chopped fresh dill
½ teaspoon Turkish red pepper or ground red pepper
4 tablespoons lemon juice
Salt and freshly ground black pepper
Bread cubes toasted with olive oil (optional, see note)

Place the fish chunks and stock in a large saucepan. Bring it to a boil; then lower the heat and simmer for about 12 minutes.

Using a slotted spoon, remove the fish from the saucepan. Chop it finely, removing any bones, and set it aside. Strain the stock into a bowl and set aside.

Heat the oil in a large heavy saucepan. Add the onion and garlic and cook them gently, stirring frequently with a wooden spoon, for about 2 minutes, until they're softened but not brown. Add the reserved fish stock, potatoes, carrots, celery, and tomatoes. Stir well and bring the mixture to a boil, then lower the heat, cover the saucepan, and simmer for about 20 minutes, or until the vegetables are tender.

Add the fish to the saucepan along with the chopped parsley and dill, Turkish pepper, and lemon juice. Season with salt and pepper. Stir gently and cook for another 5 minutes.

Ladle the soup into individual bowls and top with bread cubes toasted with olive oil, if so desired. Serve at once.

NOTE: To make the bread cubes, dice a few slices of white bread. Heat olive oil in a saucepan, add the bread cubes, and cook them, tossing the pan to coat the cubes evenly, until they are golden. Alternatively, toast them in the broiler for 2 to 3 minutes, but watch them carefully so they do not burn.

~~~~~~~~~~~~~~~~

Ezogelin Çorbası

Red Lentil, Bulgur, and Mint Soup

SERVES 4–6

Sultan's Kitchen presented this soup to more than 1500 guests at the annual James Beard Awards Dinner in May 1995.

2 tablespoons virgin olive oil
2 tablespoons unsalted clarified butter (page 7)
1 large Spanish onion, finely diced (¾ cup)
2 garlic cloves, minced
2 tablespoons tomato paste
1 medium tomato, peeled, seeded, and finely
  chopped (½ cup)
2 tablespoons paprika
½ teaspoon Turkish red pepper or ground red pepper
1½ cups red lentils
¼ cup long-grain white rice
6 cups chicken stock (page 58) or water
¼ cup fine-grain bulgur
1 tablespoon dried mint
Salt and freshly ground black pepper
Plain bread croutons (optional)
Lemon wedges

TOPPING
2 tablespoons unsalted butter
1 teaspoon dried mint
½ teaspoon paprika

In a heavy medium-size saucepan, heat the olive oil and the butter over medium heat. Add the onion and garlic and cook gently for about 2 minutes, or until they're softened but not brown. Stir in the tomato paste, chopped tomato, paprika, and Turkish pepper. Add the lentils, rice, and stock. Cover the saucepan and bring the liquid to a boil. Lower the heat and simmer for 30 to 35 minutes, stirring occasionally, until the rice is cooked and the lentils have blended with the stock. Add the bulgur and mint, and season with salt and pepper. Cook for another 10 minutes, stirring occasionally. If the soup is too thick, add a little water.

To make the topping, melt the butter in a small saucepan over low heat, add the mint and paprika, and stir the mixture until it sizzles. Ladle the soup into individual bowls and drizzle the butter mixture over each serving. Top with the croutons, if you're using them. Serve at once with lemon wedges.

~ Red Lentil, Bulgur, and Mint Soup

~~~~~~~~~~~~~~~~

Arpa Şehriyeli Domates Çorbası

Tomato with Orzo Soup

SERVES 4–6

This somewhat fruity, red soup is another of my favorites. It is best made with vine-ripened tomatoes.

As a variation, sprinkle each bowl with croutons and some grated kasseri cheese, then place it under the broiler until the cheese is melted. Take it out and drizzle a little olive oil on top.

2 tablespoons virgin olive oil
2 tablespoons unsalted clarified butter (page 7)
1 small Spanish onion, chopped (1/2 cup)
2 pounds tomatoes, peeled, seeded, and
    chopped (4 cups)
2 tablespoons tomato paste (optional)
1 sprig fresh thyme or 1/4 teaspoon dried
Pinch of sugar (optional)
1 small green bell pepper, chopped (1/2 cup)
1 celery rib, chopped
4 cups chicken stock (page 58) or water
1/4 cup orzo
1/4 cup heavy cream
Salt and freshly ground white pepper
3 ounces grated kasseri cheese (1/3 cup)

In a heavy medium-size saucepan, heat the oil and the butter together over medium heat. Add the onion and cook gently for about 2 minutes, stirring, until it's softened but not brown. Add the chopped tomatoes, tomato paste, thyme, and a pinch of sugar (if you're using it), and mix together. Add the green peppers, celery, and stock, stirring constantly. Bring the liquid to a boil; then lower the heat and simmer for about 30 minutes.

Pass the soup through a fine sieve, pressing the mixture with the back of a wooden spoon to extract the juices from the vegetables. Discard the vegetables and return the soup to the saucepan. Add the orzo and cook gently for 25 minutes, stirring occasionally, until the orzo is cooked. Stir in the cream and season with salt and white pepper. Cook for another 5 minutes, making sure the soup does not come to a boil.

Ladle the soup into individual serving bowls. Sprinkle with grated kasseri cheese and serve.

Note: If you find the color is not deep enough, use tomato paste to redden it.

~~~~~~~~~~~~~~~~~

Kara Lahana Çorbası

Collard Green Soup

SERVES 4–6

This soup from northern Turkey will warm you on chilly winter days.

1/4 cup unsalted clarified butter (page 7)
1 small Spanish onion, finely diced (1/2 cup)
2 garlic cloves, minced
3/4 pound lean ground beef
1 tablespoon tomato paste
2 large tomatoes, peeled, seeded, and finely diced
    (1 1/2 cups)
3/4 cup great northern beans or small lima beans,
    soaked and drained (page 7)
6 cups beef stock
1 pound collard greens, trimmed (include tender stems)
    and coarsely chopped (about 3 cups)
1/4 cup orzo
4 sprigs fresh Italian parsley, trimmed and coarsely
    chopped
1/2 teaspoon Turkish red pepper or ground red pepper
Salt

Heat the butter in a heavy medium-size saucepan over medium heat. Add the onion and garlic, and cook gently for 2 minutes, stirring, until they're softened but not brown. Add the ground beef and cook for 2 minutes to brown all over. Stir in the tomato paste, tomatoes, and beans. Add the stock, cover the saucepan, and bring the mixture to a boil, then lower the heat and simmer for about 30 minutes, stirring occasionally.

Add the cabbage, orzo, parsley, and Turkish pepper. Season with salt and cook for another 30 minutes, stirring frequently, until the beans are tender but not falling apart and the cabbage is softened. Pour the soup into individual bowls and serve at once.

~~~~~~~~~~~~~~~~~~

Düğün Çorbası

Wedding Soup

SERVES 4–6

This hearty soup is traditionally served at village weddings. It also makes a warming dish during the cold winter months. The ingredients vary slightly from region to region.

NOTE: To prepare this recipe, you will need to soak all of the beans except for the lentils. See page 7 for instructions.

> 1/2 cup dried lima beans, soaked overnight and drained
> 1/2 cup dried chickpeas, soaked overnight and drained
> 1/2 cup dried black-eyed peas, soaked overnight and drained
> 1/2 cup green lentils
> 1/4 cup unsalted clarified butter (page 7), divided
> 3/4 pound trimmed boneless shoulder of lamb or lamb shank, cut into 1/2 inch chunks
> 1 Spanish onion, finely diced (1/2 cup)
> 3 garlic cloves, minced
> 1 quart lamb stock (page 60)
> 2 carrots, diced (3/4 cup)
> 2 celery ribs, diced (3/4 cup)
> 2 leeks, trimmed and sliced (white parts only) (3/4 cup)
> Salt and freshly ground black pepper
> 4 egg yolks
> 2 tablespoons all-purpose flour
> 2 tablespoons lemon juice
> 1/2 teaspoon Turkish red pepper or ground red pepper
> 1 1/2 tablespoons paprika

Bring 1 1/2 quarts water to a boil in a medium-size saucepan over high heat. Add the lima beans, chickpeas, and black-eyed peas. Lower the heat, cover the saucepan, and simmer for 40 minutes. Add the green lentils and cook for another 20 minutes, stirring occasionally with a wooden spoon, until the peas and beans are tender. Add a little more water during cooking if the water level goes below half the depth of the beans. Drain the mixture and reserve the liquid.

Heat 2 tablespoons of the butter in a heavy medium-size saucepan over medium heat. Using a wooden spoon, stir in the lamb, onion, and garlic and cook for about 5 minutes. Add the stock, cover the saucepan, and bring the mixture to a boil; then lower the heat and simmer the mixture for about 30 minutes. Add the carrot, celery, and leeks and cook for another 10 minutes. Add the cooked beans along with 2 cups of the reserved cooking liquid. Season with salt and pepper.

Mix the egg yolks, flour, and lemon juice in a bowl. Gently ladle 1 cup of the hot lamb soup into the bowl and blend well. Then slowly stir this egg mixture back into the soup. Cook the soup very gently for 5 minutes.

Just before serving the soup, melt the remaining butter in a small pan, and add the Turkish pepper and paprika, stirring the mixture until it sizzles. Drizzle the hot butter over each serving. Serve at once.

~~~~~~~~~~~~~~~~~~

Tarhana

Tarhana Dough
MAKES 8 CUPS

Tarhana is a grainy fermented dough that is used to make a hearty winter soup (page 73). In Turkey, people dry tarhana dough outdoors in the sun. The dough is draped over balconies and on flat rooftops. In the villages of Selçuk and Ephesus, it is left to dry on ancient marble ruins for as long as ten days. The colorful red dough is a wonderful sight, and its tangy, slightly hot taste makes it well worth making. Ready-made Turkish tarhana is sold in small packages in Middle Eastern supermarkets.

It will take you about ten days to make this dough because it needs to dry slowly and completely. This recipe makes more dough than is needed for one recipe of Village Soup, but the dried dough will keep for up to a year refrigerated in a cloth bag.

1 cup dried chickpeas, or 1½ cups cooked chickpeas
1 medium Spanish onion, coarsely chopped (³/4 cup)
2 tomatoes, peeled, seeded, and coarsely chopped (1½ cups)
2 small red hot chile peppers, seeded and coarsely chopped (½ cup)
2 large sweet red peppers, seeded and coarsely chopped (1½ cups)
Salt
2 cups thick yogurt (see *süzme* yogurt on page 11)
5 cups all-purpose flour, sifted, plus extra for dusting
¼ cup virgin olive oil
1 tablespoon dried mint
1 tablespoon dried dill
Salt

Place 1 cup water, the chickpeas, onion, tomatoes, hot pepper, and sweet pepper in a heavy medium-sized saucepan. Lightly season with salt. Bring to a boil, then lower the heat and simmer for about 30 minutes, or until all the water has been absorbed. Remove the mixture from the heat and let it cool.

Add the yogurt, flour, olive oil, mint, and dill to the cooled mixture. Season again with salt and blend well.

On a lightly floured work surface, turn out the mixture and knead it well for about 5 minutes, dusting your hands and the mixture with flour, to make a slightly moist dough. Cover the dough, and let it stand at room temperature for three days, during which time the dough will ferment. Knead the dough for 5 minutes each day.

On the fourth day, divide the dough into small pieces and shape it into balls—each about 2 inches in diameter (Figure 1). Place them on a lightly floured cloth in a warm place or in an oven with a pilot light, leaving the door ajar. Let the balls of dough rest until their outsides have dried (it should take about a day, but it may take longer).

Flatten each dried ball, divide it in half, and shape it into two smaller balls. Repeat this process—letting the dough dry on the outside, flattening each ball, dividing it in half, and reshaping it into two balls—three more times over the course of several days (Figure 2).

Place the dried balls of dough in a sieve held over a lightly floured baking pan. Push the dough through the sieve (Figure 3), and with your fingertips crumble and spread the dough to make very small pieces, about the size of small grains. Let the grains stand in a cool place for another four days until they're completely dry. Place them in an airtight container and refrigerate until you're ready to use them.

~ Steps for making tarhana dough

~ Figure 1

~ Figure 2

~ Figure 3

~~~~~~~~~~~~~~~~~

Tarhana Çorbası

Village Soup

SERVES 4–6

This recipe was given to me by my mother.

1 cup tarhana (page 70)
1½ quarts chicken stock (page 58) or water, divided
¼ cup unsalted clarified butter (page 7)
1 tablespoon tomato paste
Salt
Croutons (optional)

TOPPING
2 tablespoons unsalted butter
1 teaspoon Turkish red pepper or ground red pepper
1½ teaspoons dried mint

Soak the tarhana in 1 cup chicken stock for 30 minutes.

Heat the butter in a heavy medium-size saucepan over medium heat. Stir in the tomato paste and remaining chicken stock. Bring the mixture to a boil, stirring constantly, then lower the heat and add the tarhana with chicken stock. Season with salt. Simmer the mixture for about 10 minutes. If the soup is too thick, add a little more water.

To make the topping, melt the butter in a small saucepan. Add the Turkish pepper and mint. Stir the mixture until it sizzles. Ladle the soup into individual bowls and drizzle the hot butter mixture over each serving. Serve at once.

~ Village Soup

~~~~~~~~~~~~~~~~~

İşkembe Çorbası

Tripe Soup

SERVES 4–6

The rough texture of tripe gives this soup its heartiness, and the warming, tangy flavors of garlic, pepper, and lemon absorbed by the tripe during long, slow cooking make this soup popular in Turkey for late-night or very early morning dining.

2 pounds beef tripe, washed and drained
6 garlic cloves, chopped, divided
¼ cup lemon juice
⅓ cup virgin olive oil
Salt
¼ cup (½ stick) unsalted butter
⅓ cup all-purpose flour
1 cup milk
¼ cup white wine vinegar
2 teaspoons Turkish red pepper or ground red pepper

Place the tripe, 4 cloves of the garlic, the lemon juice, olive oil, and 2 quarts water in a large heavy saucepan. Season with salt. Bring the mixture to a boil; then cover the saucepan and simmer for about 4 hours, or until the tripe is soft. Add extra water as needed to keep the tripe submerged. Skim off any scum that rises to the surface.

Remove the tripe from the saucepan and let it cool. Reserve 1½ quarts cooking liquid—add a little extra water if necessary. Cut the tripe into ½-inch pieces.

In a separate saucepan, melt the butter over medium heat. Use a wooden spoon to stir in the flour, and cook the mixture for 2 minutes, stirring constantly. Gradually stir in the cooking liquid, then add the milk and tripe pieces. Stir well and simmer the mixture for about 30 minutes.

To serve, mix the vinegar, Turkish red pepper, and remaining garlic in a small bowl.

Ladle the soup into individual bowls and spoon some of the vinegar mixture onto each serving. Serve at once.

LAMB, BEEF, AND CHICKEN

~~~~~~~~~~~~~~~~~~~~~~

WHEN MEAT IS DISCUSSED IN TURKISH cuisine, what is usually meant is lamb, which is eaten far oftener than any other kind of meat. Lamb is prepared in a multitude of different ways. It can be cut into chunks, marinated, and grilled directly over a charcoal fire as in Izgara Kuzu Şiş Kebabı (page 92) or stewed in a clay pot with vegetables as in Kuzu Etli Kuru Fasülye Güveci (page 81). It can be roasted (page 82), rolled in swiss chard and braised (page 84), or ground and mixed with spices to make *köfte* (kofta).

Almost every city in Turkey has its own style of kofta, which always consists of spiced, ground lamb, but sometimes takes the form of meatballs that are baked (like the İzmir Köftesi on page 77) or cooked on a hot griddle, and sometimes it is pressed onto skewers and grilled (like the Baharatlı Izgara Şiş Kebabı on page 77). Paşa Köftesi (page 76), large spiced meatballs served with creamy garlic mashed potatoes, are yet another example of koftas.

Perhaps the most succulent of lamb dishes (which I haven't included here) is Kuyu or Tandır Kebabı, which is prepared by slowly cooking an entire baby lamb in a brick oven or in a six-foot-deep pit oven.

A very special Turkish dish was made famous years ago by the visiting Empress Eugénie, the wife of Napoleon III, who so enjoyed a smoky creamed eggplant dish topped with chunks of well-seasoned lamb that she requested the recipe. This dish, called Hünkar Beğendi (page 87), is still enjoyed today: as the story goes, the empress's chef went down to the kitchen to get the exact recipe on paper. The palace chef told him that a true chef does not cook from exact recipes but from instinct. Somehow the empress never did get the recipe.

Chicken is also popular in Turkey, especially during the summer months, when it is cooked with seasonal vegetables—baby okra, eggplants, tomatoes, and green peppers.

NOTE: To prepare some dishes, you will need long, flat skewers, 15 inches long and 1/2 inch wide. If you can't find them, use regular skewers, but be sure to pack the meat on well so it doesn't fall off the skewer when you cook it.

~~~~~~~~~~~~~~~~~

Paşa Köftesi

Pasha's Kofta

SERVES 4

This is a wonderful dish for winter: the creamy garlic mashed potatoes are mounded in the center of the large meat balls. It is nice served with a salad. I prepared this dish on the TV Food Network, July 5, 1995.

4 slices day-old white bread, crusts removed
2 pounds lean ground lamb or beef
1/2 small Spanish onion, grated (1/4 cup)
4 garlic cloves, minced
1/4 cup finely chopped fresh Italian parsley
2 eggs
1/2 teaspoon Turkish red pepper or ground red pepper
1 teaspoon paprika
1 tablespoon ground cumin
Salt and freshly ground black pepper

CREAMY GARLIC MASHED POTATOES
1/3 cup milk
2 tablespoons heavy cream
1 pound potatoes, peeled and cut into large chunks
    (11/2 cups)
2 tablespoons unsalted butter
2 garlic cloves, minced
Salt and freshly ground white pepper
4 ounces grated kasseri cheese (1/2 cup)
3 tablespoons unsalted butter
1 tablespoon tomato paste
4 medium tomatoes, peeled, seeded, and chopped
    (21/2 cups)
2 cups lamb stock (page 58) or water
1 tablespoon finely chopped fresh Italian parsley

Heat the oven to 350°F.

To make the kofta: soak the bread in cold water briefly and squeeze out the excess water. Combine the lamb or beef, bread, onion, garlic, parsley, eggs, Turkish red pepper, paprika, and cumin in a large bowl. Season with salt and pepper. Moisten your hands and mix the ingredients for about 2 minutes. Cover the bowl and refrigerate for about 30 minutes.

To make the mashed potatoes, heat the milk and cream in a small saucepan until it is just warm. Set this mixture aside and

keep it warm. Put the potatoes in a large saucepan and cover them with lightly salted water. Bring the pan to a boil over high heat, lower the heat to medium, and cook the potatoes for about 15 minutes, or until they're tender. Make sure they do not overcook. Drain them well.

Place the butter and garlic in a saucepan set over low heat, stirring for about 1 minute, until the butter has melted. Add the potatoes and the warm milk-and-cream mixture. Season with salt and white pepper. Mash the mixture with a potato masher for about 1 minute until the potatoes are smooth and creamy.

Using moistened hands, divide the chilled meat mixture into 4 equal portions, shaping each into a round ball. Flatten each one slightly and make a well in the center of each one. Arrange the koftas in an ovenproof baking dish. Place equal amounts of the creamy garlic mashed potatoes in the center well of each one. Sprinkle with kasseri cheese.

In a small saucepan, melt the butter over medium heat and stir in the tomato paste. Add the tomatoes and stock, bring the mixture to a boil, and boil for 3 minutes, stirring constantly. The sauce will reduce a bit. Pour this sauce around the koftas—do not pour sauce over the potatoes. Bake, uncovered, for about 35 minutes, or until the top of the potatoes is lightly browned.

Arrange the koftas in the center of warmed plates. Spoon the sauce around them and sprinkle them with parsley. Serve at once.

~ Spicy Char-Grilled Kofta Shish Kebab (page 77)

~~~~~~~~~~~~~~~~~~~

Baharatlı Izgara Köfte Şiş Kebabı

Spicy Char-Grilled Kofta Shish Kebab

SERVES 4

Baharat is a spice mixture. In this recipe it consists of Turkish pepper, sumac, and paprika, but it can also include ground oregano, ground cinnamon, ground cloves, black pepper, ginger, garlic, and mint.

NOTE: To prepare this dish you will need four long, flat skewers. See the note on page 74.

4 slices day-old bread, crusts removed
2 pounds ground lean lamb or beef
1/2 small Spanish onion, grated (1/4 cup)
4 garlic cloves, minced
2 eggs
2 teaspoons Turkish red pepper or ground red pepper
1 teaspoon ground sumac
1 teaspoon paprika
1 tablespoon ground cumin
1/4 cup finely chopped fresh Italian parsley
Salt and freshly ground black pepper

Prepare a charcoal grill.

To make the kofta: soak the bread in cold water briefly and squeeze out the excess water. Combine the lamb or beef, bread, onion, garlic, eggs, Turkish red pepper, sumac, paprika, cumin, and parsley in a large bowl. Season with salt and pepper. With moistened hands, mix the ingredients for about 2 minutes. Cover the bowl and refrigerate for about 30 minutes.

With moistened hands—keep a bowl of warm water nearby—divide the chilled meat mixture into 4 equal portions. Hold a skewer upright with one hand, and with the other hand form the meat into a sausage shape onto the skewer. Start at the lower end of the skewer and work your way to the tip of the skewer by gently pressing the meat against it, opening and closing the palm of your hand with a continuous, quick motion.

Place the koftas on the hot grill set 5 inches above the coals. Grill the meat for about 8 minutes, turning frequently, until it's cooked through. Pull the skewer out of each kofta and serve at once.

~~~~~~~~~~~~~~~~~~~

İzmir Köftesi

Kofta in Tomato Sauce

SERVES 4

This recipe is from the Aegean city of İzmir. Serve it with lightly fried potatoes and a salad.

4 slices day-old white bread, crusts removed
2 pounds lean ground lamb or beef
1/2 small Spanish onion, grated (1/4 cup)
4 garlic cloves, minced
2 eggs
1 teaspoon paprika
1 tablespoon ground cumin
1/4 cup finely chopped fresh Italian parsley
Salt and freshly ground black pepper
1/4 cup virgin olive oil
2 tablespoons unsalted butter
1 tablespoon tomato paste
3 large tomatoes, peeled, seeded, and finely
    chopped (2 cups)
2 cups lamb stock (page 58) or water
Salt and freshly ground black pepper
2 medium Italian green peppers, seeded and cut
    diagonally into slices

Heat the oven to 350°F.

To make the kofta: soak the bread in cold water briefly and squeeze out the excess water. Combine the ground lamb or beef, bread, onion, garlic, eggs, paprika, cumin, and Italian parsley in a large bowl. Season with salt and pepper. With moistened hands, mix the ingredients for about 2 minutes. Keep a bowl of warm water nearby to wet your hands while working. Shape the meat mixture into 16 oval balls.

Heat the oil in a large skillet over high heat, add the kofta balls, and lightly brown the meat all over (about 5 minutes). Place the koftas in an ovenproof dish and set them aside.

Melt the butter in a small saucepan. Stir in the tomato paste, then add the tomatoes and lamb stock. Season with salt and pepper. Bring the mixture to a boil, stirring. Pour this sauce over the koftas. Arrange the green peppers on top. Cover the dish and bake for 40 minutes. To check for doneness, cut one kofta open; the meat should be brown, not pink. Serve at once.

~~~~~~~~~~~~~~~

Yoğurtlu Kebap

**Kofta Kebabs with Tomato Sauce
and Yogurt-Garlic Sauce**

SERVES 4

This is one of the most popular dishes we serve at Sultan's Kitchen; I demonstrated its preparation on the TV Food Network in 1995. To prepare this dish, you will need four long, flat skewers—see the note on page 74. You can substitute cubed lamb for the ground lamb if you prefer.

KOFTA

4 slices day-old white bread, crusts
removed
2 pounds lean ground lamb or beef
1/2 small Spanish onion, grated (1/4 cup)
4 garlic cloves, minced
2 eggs
1 tablespoon paprika, plus 1 teaspoon
1 tablespoon ground cumin
1/3 cup finely chopped fresh Italian
parsley, plus 1 tablespoon
Salt and freshly ground black pepper

TOMATO SAUCE

1 1/2 tablespoons virgin olive oil
4 large tomatoes, peeled, seeded,
and finely chopped (2 1/2 cups)
Salt and freshly ground black pepper

2 pita breads
1 recipe Yogurt-Garlic Sauce (page 13)
1/4 cup (1 stick) unsalted butter
1/2 teaspoon Turkish red pepper or
ground red pepper

To make the kofta, soak the bread in cold water briefly, then squeeze the excess water out. Combine the lamb or beef, bread, onion, garlic, eggs, 1 tablespoon paprika, cumin, and 1/3 cup parsley in a large bowl. Season with salt and pepper and mix together, using your hands to mix the ingredients for about 2 minutes. Cover and refrigerate the meat for about 30 minutes.

To make the sauce, heat the olive oil in a small saucepan over medium heat and stir in the tomatoes. Cook for about 1 minute, mashing the tomatoes with a potato masher or a fork, until they form a puree. Season with salt and pepper. Keep the sauce warm.

Prepare a charcoal grill.

With moistened hands—keep a bowl of warm water nearby—divide the chilled meat mixture into 4 equal portions. Hold a skewer upright with one hand, and with the other hand form the meat into a sausage shape on the skewer. Start at the lower end and work your way to the tip of the skewer by gently pressing the meat against it, opening and closing your hand with a continuous, quick motion.

Place the koftas on a hot grill set 5 inches above the coals. Grill the meat for about 4 minutes on each side for medium-cooked meat, 6 minutes on each side for well done. Turn the meat frequently during cooking.

While the koftas are grilling, warm the pita bread and cut it into 1-inch cubes. Divide the bread among 4 warmed plates.

Pull out the skewer from each kofta and cut each one into 4 or 5 slices. Place the slices on top of the pita bread. Spoon the warm tomato sauce over the meat and top it with the yogurt-garlic sauce.

Melt the butter in a small pan and stir in 1 teaspoon paprika, 1 tablespoon parsley, and the Turkish red pepper. Drizzle this mixture over the yogurt-garlic sauce. Serve at once.

~ Kofta Kebabs with Tomato Sauce and
Yogurt-Garlic Sauce

~~~~~~~~~~~~~~~~

Kuzu Etli Terbiyeli Kereviz Bastısı

Lamb with Celeriac

SERVES 4–6

Serve this dish with rice pilaf and salad.

> 6 tablespoons all-purpose flour, divided
> 3 tablespoons lemon juice
> 2 medium-size celeriac knobs
> 1 lemon, cut in half
> 1/4 cup (1/2 stick) unsalted butter
> 2 to 2 1/2 pounds boneless lamb shoulder or shank,
>   trimmed of excess fat and cut into 1 1/2-inch chunks.
> 1 large Spanish onion, diced (3/4 cup)
> 2 cups lamb stock (page 58) or water
> 1 tablespoon finely chopped fresh dill
> Salt and freshly ground black pepper
> 2 egg yolks
> 1 tablespoon cornstarch

Blend 3 tablespoons of the flour and 3 tablespoons lemon juice with 1 quart cold water. Peel the celeriac and cut it into 1-inch-thick slices. Rub the slices all over with half of the cut lemon, place them in the water and flour mixture to help prevent discoloration, and set them aside.

Melt the butter in a heavy medium-size saucepan and brown the lamb chunks all over for about 6 minutes over high heat, stirring frequently with a wooden spoon. Stir in the onion and cook for 1 minute more, stirring. Add the stock, cover the saucepan, and bring the mixture to a boil. Lower the heat and simmer for about 50 minutes, skimming the surface occasionally to remove any scum that rises to the top.

Shake off the excess water from the celeriac slices and arrange them in a flameproof casserole dish. Remove the lamb from the heat and transfer it to the dish. Add the dill and season with salt and pepper. Press a flameproof plate on top of the lamb mixture (make sure the plate fits inside the casserole dish). Cover the dish and simmer over low to medium heat for about 20 minutes or until the lamb is cooked through and the celeriac is tender.

Remove the casserole dish from the heat and ladle the cooking liquid into a small saucepan. Blend the remaining flour with 3 tablespoons water. Add this thickening agent to the saucepan.

Bring the mixture to a boil, stirring occasionally; then lower the heat and simmer for about 1 minute.

Blend the egg yolks with the juice of the remaining half lemon and the cornstarch. Pour this mixture slowly into the saucepan, stirring constantly, and continue cooking the mixture for about 2 minutes until it thickens. Do not allow the sauce to boil—it may curdle. Pour this sauce over the lamb and celeriac and serve.

~~~~~~~~~~~~~~~~

Kuzu Yahnisi

Lamb Ragout with Shallots

SERVES 4

> 3 tablespoons virgin olive oil
> 2 tablespoons unsalted butter
> 2 to 2 1/2 pounds boneless lamb shoulder or shank,
>   trimmed of excess fat and cut into 1-inch chunks
> 3/4 pound small shallots, whole
> 4 garlic cloves, minced
> 2 tablespoons all-purpose flour
> 1 1/2 cups lamb stock (page 58) or water
> 1/2 cup dry red wine
> 1 1/2 teaspoons tomato paste
> 2 large tomatoes, peeled, seeded, and finely
>   chopped (1 1/2 cups)
> 2 medium Italian green peppers, seeded and
>   finely chopped (3/4 cup)
> 1/2 teaspoon Turkish red pepper or ground red pepper
> 1 tablespoon finely chopped fresh dill
> Salt and freshly ground black pepper

Heat the oven to 350°.

Heat the olive oil and melt the butter in a large heavy skillet over high heat. Brown the lamb all over, stirring with a wooden spoon, for about 6 minutes. Stir in the shallots and cook for another 2 minutes, stirring, until they're lightly browned all over. Add the garlic and sprinkle the flour all over the mixture. Pour in the stock and red wine. Add the tomato paste, tomatoes, green peppers, Turkish red pepper, and dill. Season with salt and pepper and stir to blend. Bring the mixture to a boil, skimming the surface occasionally to remove any scum that rises to the top.

Transfer the mixture to an ovenproof dish. Cover the dish and bake in the oven for about 1 hour, or until the meat is tender. Transfer the mixture to warmed plates and serve.

~~~~~~~~~~~~~~~~~~~

Kuzu Etli Kuru Fasülye Güveci

Lamb with White Beans in a Clay Pot

SERVES 4–6

This is a typical Turkish dish that is eaten throughout the year. It tastes best when it is prepared the traditional way, in a clay pot, and the flavors develop if you let them blend overnight and eat it the next day. If you don't have a clay pot, use a covered casserole dish. Serve it with White Rice Pilaf (page 115) and Cucumbers with Yogurt and Mint (page 36).

> 1/4 cup (1/2 stick) unsalted butter
> 2 to 2 1/2 pounds boneless lamb shoulder or shank, trimmed of excess fat and cut into 1-inch cubes
> 1 medium Spanish onion, diced (1/4 cup)
> 4 garlic cloves, minced
> 1 tablespoon tomato paste
> 4 medium tomatoes, peeled, seeded, and coarsely chopped (2 1/2 cups)
> 2 cups great northern beans, soaked overnight and drained (page 7)
> 1 teaspoon Turkish red pepper or ground red pepper
> 2 cups lamb stock (page 58) or water
> Salt and freshly ground black pepper
> 3 medium Italian green peppers, seeded and chopped crosswise (1 cup)
> 1/4 cup coarsely chopped Italian parsley

In a heavy medium-size saucepan, melt the butter over high heat. Add the lamb chunks and brown the meat all over for about 6 minutes, stirring with a wooden spoon. Add the onion and garlic and cook for 1 minute more, then add the tomato paste, tomatoes, beans, Turkish red pepper, and stock. Season with salt and pepper. Cover the saucepan and simmer for 45 minutes, skimming the surface occasionally to remove any scum that rises to the top.

Heat the oven to 350°F.

Transfer the mixture to a clay pot. Add the green peppers. Cover the pot and cook in the oven for 1 hour or until the beans are tender but not mushy. Garnish with chopped parsley and serve.

~~~~~~~~~~~~~~~~~~~

Kuzu Etli Bamya

Lamb with Okra

SERVES 4–6

This is my favorite dish during the summer months, when okra is plentiful in Turkey. There you can buy okra very small (about 3/4 inch long). You can obtain small okra frozen and canned in Middle Eastern groceries. You may also substitute larger okra.

> 1 1/2 pounds small okra
> 1/2 cup lemon juice, divided
> 3 tablespoons unsalted butter
> 3 tablespoons virgin olive oil
> 2 to 2 1/2 pounds boneless lamb shoulder or shank, trimmed of excess fat and cut into 1-inch chunks
> 1 small Spanish onion, finely diced (1/2 cup)
> 4 garlic cloves, minced
> 1 tablespoon tomato paste
> 4 medium tomatoes, peeled, seeded, and finely chopped (2 1/2 cups)
> 2 cups lamb stock (page 58) or water
> Salt and freshly ground black pepper
> 1/4 teaspoon Turkish red pepper or ground red pepper
> 1 tablespoon dried mint

Gently pare around the cone-shaped tops of the okras. Place them in a bowl and sprinkle them with salt and just over half the lemon juice. Toss well and set them aside for at least 20 minutes.

Melt the butter and heat the oil in a heavy medium-size saucepan over high heat. Brown the lamb chunks, stirring with a wooden spoon, for about 6 minutes. Add the onion and garlic and cook them gently, stirring, for 1 minute. Add the tomato paste, tomatoes, and stock. Season with salt and pepper. Bring the mixture to a boil; then lower the heat, cover the saucepan, and simmer for about 45 minutes, skimming the surface occasionally to remove any scum that rises to the top.

Drain the okras and rinse them well under cold running water. Add them to the saucepan of cooked lamb along with the Turkish red pepper and mint. Cover the saucepan and simmer for another 25 minutes, or until the lamb is tender. Stir in the remaining lemon juice. Serve hot or warm.

~~~~~~~~~~~~~~~~~

Kuzu Kol Sarması

Stuffed, Rolled, and Roasted Shoulder of Lamb

SERVES 6

Use tender spring lamb for this dish for the best flavor. In Turkey, lamb is eaten medium-rare, so the cooking time I've given here is for medium-rare lamb—leave it in a little longer if you like it well done.

6 ounces fresh spinach leaves, trimmed
1 large carrot, cut into quarters lengthwise
3 pounds boneless square-cut lamb shoulder, trimmed of excess fat
3 tablespoons virgin olive oil
8 garlic cloves, divided
1/2 small Spanish onion, grated (1/4 cup)
1 tablespoon ground cumin
1/2 teaspoon fresh thyme
2 teaspoons fresh oregano
Salt and freshly ground black pepper
3 large tomatoes, peeled, seeded, and finely chopped (2 cups)
1 1/2 cups lamb stock (page 58)
1/4 cup finely chopped fresh Italian parsley

Heat the oven to 375°F.

In a large saucepan, bring 4 quarts lightly salted water to a boil and blanch the spinach for about 15 seconds. Remove the spinach from the saucepan and drain well. When it's cool enough to handle, squeeze out the excess water and chop the spinach coarsely. Set it aside.

In the same pan of boiling water, blanch the carrot quarters for about 4 minutes, remove them from the saucepan, and set them aside.

Place the lamb on a work surface, skin side down. Brush the flesh with olive oil. Mince 2 of the garlic cloves and rub them and the grated onion over the lamb flesh. Sprinkle with the cumin, thyme, and oregano. Season with salt and pepper. Lay the spinach in the center of the lamb. Place the carrots on top of the spinach. Bring both ends of the lamb toward the center, up over the spinach and carrots. Tie the lamb together tightly with kitchen string.

Place the rolled lamb in a roasting pan with the remaining garlic cloves, the tomatoes, and stock. Season with salt and pepper. Cover the pan and roast the lamb for 1 hour 10 minutes, basting it occasionally with the liquid in the bottom of the pan. Remove the cover and roast for another 10 minutes to brown the surface of the meat. For well-done meat, add 15 more minutes to the cooking time.

Transfer the meat to a work surface and loosely cover it with foil. Strain the cooking liquid into a small saucepan and boil this sauce until it has reduced and thickened slightly. Season with salt and pepper.

Cut the lamb into thin slices. Spoon the sauce onto warmed plates and arrange the meat on top. Place the garlic cloves around the meat, sprinkle with parsley, and serve.

~~~~~~~~~~~~~~~~~

Baharatlı Kuzu Budu Fırında

Roast Leg of Lamb with Herbs and Spices

SERVES 6

This dish can be made with a 5-pound leg of lamb with the bone in. A boneless leg is much easier to slice, but the lamb is tastier on the bone. It also makes a more dramatic presentation for guests. Rice Pilaf with Currants and Pine Nuts (page 120) is a nice accompaniment.

MARINADE
2 tablespoons virgin olive oil
1 large Spanish onion, grated (1 cup)
5 garlic cloves, minced
2 tablespoons tomato paste
1 teaspoon fresh thyme
2 teaspoons fresh oregano
2 teaspoons dried mint
1 tablespoon dried dill
1 tablespoon paprika
2 tablespoons ground cumin
1/4 cup lemon juice
1 cup plain yogurt
Salt and freshly ground black pepper

3 1/2 pounds boned leg of lamb, trimmed of excess fat and tied
1 1/2 cups lamb stock (page 58)

~ Stuffed, Rolled, and Roasted Shoulder of Lamb

Mix all the ingredients for the marinade and rub it all over the leg of lamb. Cover and refrigerate for at least 8 hours. Then let the lamb stand at room temperature for 30 minutes before roasting it.

Heat the oven to 375°F.

Place the lamb in a roasting pan with a cover and pour over the stock. Cover the pan and roast the lamb for about 1 hour 20 minutes for medium or 95 minutes for well done, basting occasionally with the liquid in the bottom of the pan. Remove the cover 15 minutes before the end of cooking to brown the surface of the meat.

Transfer the roast to a work surface, and loosely cover it with kitchen foil. Let it stand for 10 minutes. Strain the cooking juices into a small saucepan and boil this sauce gently until it has reduced and thickened. Season with salt and pepper.

Cut the lamb into thin slices. Spoon some of the sauce onto 6 warmed plates and arrange the lamb slices on top. Spoon any remaining sauce over the meat and serve at once.

~~~~~~~~~~~~~~~~~

Kuzu Tas Kebabı ile Kremalı Sarmısaklı Patates Püresi

Stewed Lamb Kebab with Creamy Garlic Mashed Potatoes

SERVES 6

1/4 cup (1/2 stick) unsalted butter
3 pounds boneless lamb shoulder or shank, trimmed of
    excess fat and cut into 1-inch chunks
1 medium Spanish onion, diced (3/4 cup)
4 garlic cloves, minced
1 1/2 tablespoons tomato paste
4 large tomatoes, peeled, seeded, and coarsely
    chopped (2 1/2 cups)
1 teaspoon dried thyme
2 cups lamb stock (page 58) or water
2 medium carrots, cut into 1/2-inch dice (3/4 cup)
1/2 cup fresh or frozen green peas
3 medium Italian green peppers, seeded and finely
    chopped (1 cup)
Salt and freshly ground black pepper
1/4 cup finely chopped fresh Italian parsley

CREAMY GARLIC MASHED POTATOES
3/4 cup milk
1/3 cup heavy cream
3 pounds peeled potatoes, cut into large
    chunks (4 1/2 cups)
1/2 cup (1 stick) unsalted butter
6 garlic cloves, minced
Ground white pepper

Melt the butter in a heavy medium-size saucepan and brown the lamb all over for about 6 minutes over high heat, stirring frequently with a wooden spoon. Stir in the onion and garlic and cook for 1 more minute, stirring; then stir in the tomato paste and chopped tomatoes, thyme, and stock. Bring the mixture to a boil, then lower the heat, cover the saucepan, and simmer for about 30 minutes, skimming the surface occasionally to remove any scum that rises to the top. Add the carrots, peas, and green peppers and mix in. Season with salt and pepper. Continue cooking for another 20 minutes, or until the lamb is tender.

Meanwhile, make the mashed potatoes. Place the milk and cream in a small saucepan and heat until the mixture is just warm. Set it aside and keep it warm.

Put the potatoes in a large saucepan covered with lightly salted water and bring them to a boil. Lower the heat to medium and cook the potatoes for about 15 minutes, or until they're tender. Make sure they do not overcook. Remove them from the heat and drain them well.

Place the butter and garlic in a medium-size saucepan set over low heat and stir for about 1 minute until the butter has melted. Add the potatoes and the warm milk-and-cream mixture. Season with salt and white pepper. With the saucepan still over low heat, mash the potatoes for about 1 minute, until they're smooth and creamy.

Spoon the mashed potatoes onto warmed plates. Arrange the lamb kebabs on top. Sprinkle with chopped parsley and serve at once.

~~~~~~~~~~~~~~~~~

Etli Pazı Sarması

Swiss Chard Stuffed with Meat and Herbs

SERVES 4–6

STUFFING
1 medium Spanish onion, grated (3/4 cup)
4 garlic cloves, minced
1 pound ground lean lamb or beef
1 tablespoon tomato paste
2 large tomatoes, peeled, seeded, and finely chopped
    (1 1/2 cups)
1/2 cup long-grain rice
1 tablespoon finely chopped fresh dill
2 tablespoons finely chopped fresh mint
1/4 cup finely chopped fresh Italian parsley
1/2 teaspoon Turkish red pepper or ground red pepper
Salt and freshly ground black pepper

2 1/2 pounds Swiss chard
3 tablespoons unsalted butter
1 tablespoon tomato paste
2 cups lamb stock (page 58) or water
1 recipe Yogurt-Garlic Sauce (page 13)

Mix all the ingredients for the stuffing in a large bowl, until they're well blended. Cover the bowl and refrigerate.

Prepare the Swiss chard by removing the white stalks with a sharp knife. Bring 1 quart lightly salted water to a boil and blanch the Swiss chard for about 3 minutes. Using a slotted spoon, remove each leaf and plunge it into cold water to stop it from cooking. Arrange the leaves in a colander and let them drain well.

To assemble the sarmas, line up the Swiss chard leaves on a work surface, vein-side up. Cut each leaf in half lengthwise.

Place 2 tablespoons of the stuffing at one end of each leaf, fold both sides of the leaf over the stuffing, then roll up the leaf. Make sure the leaves are not folded tightly, or they may burst during cooking.

Arrange each sarma seam-side down in a flameproof casserole dish. Dot the sarmas with the butter. Blend the tomato paste with the lamb stock and add it to the casserole dish. Place crumpled wet parchment paper directly over the sarmas and set an ovenproof plate on top of the paper to weigh it down. Bring the mixture to a boil on the stovetop, then lower the heat, cover the casserole dish, and cook gently for about 1 hour 15 minutes, or until the sarmas are tender. Serve them at once with the pan juice spooned on top. Serve with yogurt-garlic sauce.

~~~~~~~~~~~~~~~~~

Etli Yaprak Sarması

Grape Leaves Stuffed with Meat and Herbs

SERVES 4–6

In the summertime, use fresh grape leaves to make these sarmas. Pick 36–40 medium-sized leaves, wash them, then poach them for about 3 minutes in boiling water seasoned with salt and lemon juice. Let them cool before you use them.

STUFFING
    1 pound ground lean lamb or beef
    1 medium Spanish onion, grated (3/4 cup)
    3 garlic cloves, minced
    1 tablespoon tomato paste
    1 medium tomato, peeled, seeded, and finely chopped
        (about 2/3 cup)
    1/2 cup long-grain rice
    2 tablespoons finely chopped fresh dill

1/4 cup chopped finely fresh Italian parsley
1/2 teaspoon Turkish red pepper or ground red pepper
Salt and freshly ground black pepper

1 (16-ounce) jar grape leaves, drained
3 tablespoons unsalted butter
1 tablespoon tomato paste
2 cups lamb stock (page 58) or water
1 recipe Yogurt-Garlic Sauce (page 13) or plain yogurt

Mix the ingredients for the stuffing in a large bowl. Season with salt and pepper and mix well. Cover and refrigerate.

To prepare the grape leaves, bring 2 quarts water to a boil, unroll the grape leaves, and place them in the boiling water for 2 minutes to soften the leaves and help rid them of the brine. Using a slotted spoon, remove the leaves from the water and drape them over the edge of a colander to drain. When cool, with a sharp knife, cut out the small protruding stem from each leaf.

To assemble the sarmas, line up 36 grape leaves side by side, vein-side up. Place 2 tablespoons of the stuffing at the stem end of each leaf. Fold the stem end over the filling, then fold both sides of the leaf in over the filling. Roll up the leaves—but not too tightly, or they may burst during cooking.

Arrange half the remaining grape leaves in the bottom of a flameproof casserole dish. Place the sarmas side by side, seam side down, on top of the leaves. Dot the sarmas with the butter. Mix the tomato paste with the stock and add this mixture to the casserole dish. Arrange the remaining grape leaves on top of the sarmas, then place crumpled wet parchment paper over the leaves and weigh it down with an ovenproof plate. Bring the liquid to a boil over medium heat on the stovetop, then lower the heat, cover the dish, and cook gently for about 1 hour 15 minutes, or until the sarmas are tender. Serve them hot with pan juices spooned on top, accompanied by yogurt-garlic sauce or plain yogurt.

N O T E : Leftover sarmas can be reheated in a covered pan set over low heat. Add a little extra lamb stock to the dish.

An alternative way to cook sarmas is to bake them in a 350° oven for 1 hour 15 minutes after you've brought the liquid to a boil on the stovetop.

~~~~~~~~~~~~~~~~~

Hünkâr Beğendi

Sultan's Delight

SERVES 6

The spiced lamb and smoky, creamy eggplant in this dish go very well together. Serve it with Shepherd's Salad (page 127).

1/4 cup (1/2 stick) unsalted butter
3 tablespoons virgin olive oil
3 pounds boneless lamb shoulder or shank,
    trimmed of excess fat and cut into 1-inch chunks
1 medium Spanish onion, diced (3/4 cup)
4 garlic cloves, minced
2 teaspoons tomato paste
4 medium tomatoes, peeled, seeded, and finely
    chopped (2 1/2 cups)
1/2 teaspoon dried thyme
1 teaspoon dried oregano
1 1/2 cups lamb stock (page 58) or water
Salt and freshly ground black pepper
1/3 cup finely chopped Italian parsley

BEĞENDI (CREAMED EGGPLANT)
3 pounds globe eggplants (about 3 large)
3 tablespoons lemon juice
3 tablespoons salt
1 cup milk
2 tablespoons heavy cream
1/4 cup (1/2 stick) unsalted butter
1/4 cup all-purpose flour
4 ounces kasseri cheese, grated (1/2 cup)

Melt the butter and heat the oil together in a heavy medium-size saucepan over high heat. Brown the lamb all over, stirring it with a wooden spoon, about 6 minutes. Add the onion and garlic and cook gently, stirring, for 1 more minute. Add the tomato paste, tomatoes, thyme, oregano, and stock. Season with salt and pepper. Bring the mixture to a boil, then lower the heat, cover the saucepan, and simmer for about 1 hour or until the lamb is tender and most of the liquid has been absorbed. Skim the surface occasionally to remove any scum that rises to the top.

While the lamb is cooking, prepare the creamed eggplant. Prepare a charcoal grill or heat the broiler. Using the tip of a skewer, prick the eggplants all over to allow the heat to penetrate. Place the eggplants on the grill, set about 5 inches above the coals, and grill them for about 15 minutes, turning occasionally, until the eggplants have collapsed completely. If you're using the broiler, broil the eggplants for about 25 minutes, turning frequently. Meanwhile, blend the lemon juice, 3 cups water, and 3 tablespoons salt in a large bowl and set it aside.

When the eggplants are cool enough to handle, peel them, and place the pulp in the bowl of lemon water. Let them stand for 10 minutes, to help prevent discoloration. Transfer the pulp to a strainer and let the excess liquid drain through by pressing the pulp gently with the back of a large wooden spoon.

In a small saucepan over low heat, mix the milk and heavy cream and heat until warm. Melt the butter in a large saucepan, then add the flour and cook gently, stirring with a wooden spoon, for about 1 minute. Using a wire whisk, slowly add the warm milk and cream, whisking constantly to incorporate the milk mixture completely, and cook gently without boiling the mixture for 1 more minute. Add the eggplant pulp and then the cheese, whisking constantly to puree the eggplant. Cook for 4 minutes, whisking, until the mixture is smooth and creamy.

Spoon the creamy eggplant onto the center of warmed plates and arrange the lamb around each serving. Top with some of the sauce from the pan of lamb. Sprinkle with chopped parsley and serve at once.

~ Sultan's Delight served with rakı, an anise-flavored liqueur

~~~~~~~~~~~~~~~~~

Etli Biber Dolması

Green Peppers Stuffed with Meat and Herbs

SERVES 6

STUFFING

 1 pound ground lean lamb or beef
 1 medium Spanish onion, grated (3/4 cup)
 4 garlic cloves, minced
 1/4 cup long-grain rice
 1 tablespoon tomato paste
 2 medium tomatoes, peeled, seeded, and finely
 chopped (1 1/2 cups)
 2 tablespoons finely chopped fresh dill
 1 tablespoon dried mint
 3/4 cup finely chopped fresh Italian parsley
 1/2 teaspoon Turkish red pepper or ground red pepper
 Salt and freshly ground black pepper

 12 small green bell peppers (about 3 pounds)
 3 medium tomatoes, quartered
 1/4 cup (1/2 stick) unsalted butter
 1 tablespoon tomato paste
 2 cups lamb stock (page 58) or water
 1 recipe Yogurt-Garlic Sauce (page 13) or plain yogurt

Mix the ingredients for the stuffing in a large bowl for about 2 minutes. Season with salt and black pepper. Cover the bowl and refrigerate while preparing the peppers.

Core and seed the green peppers. Divide the stuffing equally among the green peppers, pressing gently to fill each one. Do not overstuff the peppers, or they may burst during cooking. Press a quartered tomato on top of each stuffed pepper.

Arrange the stuffed peppers in a flameproof casserole dish, standing them upright. Dot them with the butter. Blend the tomato paste with the stock and pour this mixture over the peppers. Cover the peppers with wet crumpled parchment paper and weigh it down with an ovenproof plate. Bring the mixture to a boil over medium heat on the stovetop, then lower the heat, cover the casserole dish, and cook gently for about 45 minutes, or until the peppers are tender.

Transfer the peppers to warmed plates, pour on some of the liquid from the pan, and serve at once. Accompany the peppers with plain yogurt or yogurt-garlic sauce.

~~~~~~~~~~~~~~~~~

Etli Enginar Dolması

Artichokes Stuffed with Meat and Herbs

SERVES 6

STUFFING

 1 pound ground lean lamb or beef
 1 medium Spanish onion, grated (3/4 cup)
 4 garlic cloves, minced
 1/4 cup long-grain rice
 1 tablespoon tomato paste
 2 medium tomatoes, peeled, seeded, and finely
 chopped (1 1/2 cups)
 2 tablespoons finely chopped fresh dill
 1 tablespoon dried mint
 3/4 cup finely chopped fresh Italian parsley
 Salt and freshly ground black pepper

 1/4 cup all-purpose flour
 2 large lemons, cut in half, divided
 6 large or 12 small globe artichokes (about 4 pounds)
 1/4 cup (1/2 stick) unsalted butter
 2 cups lamb stock (page 58) or water

Place all the ingredients for the stuffing in a large bowl and mix well, until they're well blended. Cover the bowl and refrigerate it while you prepare the artichokes.

To prepare the artichokes, mix the flour and the juice from 1 1/2 lemons with 5 cups cold water in a large bowl. Cut off the stems so the artichokes stand, and trim the bottoms of the artichokes. Remove any hard outer leaves, trim off tough upper edges, scoop out the choke, and scrape it out thoroughly from the center. Rub the artichokes all over with the remaining half lemon. Place the artichokes in the bowl of lemon water to prevent discoloration.

Take each artichoke out of the bowl and shake off the excess water. Stuff it with the meat mixture, pressing gently and making sure not to overstuff it. Stand the stuffed artichokes in a flameproof casserole dish, dot them with the butter, and add the stock. Cover the artichokes with wet crumpled parchment paper and weigh it down with an ovenproof plate. Bring the liquid to a boil on the stovetop, then lower the heat, cover the casserole dish, and cook gently for about 50 minutes, or until the artichokes are tender.

Transfer the artichokes to warmed plates. Serve at once, spooning the sauce from the pot on top.

~~~~~~~~~~~~~~~~

Patlıcan Musakka

Eggplant Moussaka

SERVES 4–6

2 pounds Italian eggplant (about 6)
1/2 cup light olive oil or vegetable oil
1 cup lamb stock (page 58) or water
2 tomatoes, sliced (optional)

MEAT SAUCE

3 tablespoons unsalted butter
1 medium Spanish onion, diced (3/4 cup)
4 garlic cloves, minced
1 pound ground lean lamb or beef
1 1/2 tablespoons tomato paste
4 medium Italian green peppers, seeded and coarsely
    chopped (1 1/4 cups)
3 medium tomatoes, peeled, seeded and coarsely
    chopped (2 cups)
1/4 cup coarsely chopped fresh Italian parsley
2 teaspoons ground sumac (optional)
1 tablespoon ground cumin (optional)
Salt and freshly ground black pepper

Cut the stems off the eggplants, then peel off half of the skin in 1/2-inch, alternating, lengthwise strips to create a striped effect. Cut the eggplant into 1-inch thick round slices, and place them in a large bowl of generously salted cold water. Set the eggplant aside for 20 minutes.

Heat the oven to 350°F.

To make the meat sauce, melt the butter in a heavy saucepan over medium heat, and cook the onion and garlic for about 1 minute, or until they're softened but not brown. Using a wooden spoon, stir in the ground lamb or beef and continue cooking for another 3 minutes. Add the tomato paste, green peppers, tomatoes, parsley, and the sumac and cumin (if you're using them). Season with salt and pepper. Cook the mixture gently for 5 minutes, stirring occasionally. Remove the mixture from the heat and set it aside.

Drain and rinse the eggplant, then gently squeeze out the excess water. Pat the slices dry with paper towels. Heat the oil in a large skillet over medium heat, and fry the eggplant slices on both sides until they're lightly browned, about 2 minutes. Do not overcrowd them in the skillet and add more olive oil if necessary. Remove them from the pan and drain them on paper towels.

Spread half of the meat sauce in a baking pan. Arrange the fried eggplant slices on top and cover them with the remaining sauce. Pour over the lamb stock and bake for 25 minutes, or until the eggplant is tender. Serve warm.

~~~~~~~~~~~~~~~~

Karnıbahar Musakka

Cauliflower Moussaka

SERVES 4–6

1 large cauliflower, cut into florets
2 tablespoons unsalted butter
2 tablespoons virgin olive oil
1 medium Spanish onion, diced (3/4 cup)
4 garlic cloves, minced
1 pound ground lean lamb or beef
1 tablespoon tomato paste
2 medium Italian green peppers, seeded and
    thinly sliced
2 medium tomatoes, peeled, seeded, and finely
    chopped (1 1/2 cups)
1/2 teaspoon Turkish red pepper or ground red pepper
2 tablespoons finely chopped fresh dill
1/4 cup finely chopped fresh Italian parsley
1 1/2 cups lamb stock (page 58) or water
Salt and freshly ground black pepper
2 tablespoons lemon juice

Bring a large saucepan of lightly salted water to a boil and blanch the cauliflower florets for 4 minutes. Using a slotted spoon, remove the florets from the pan and plunge them into ice-cold water. Drain them well and set them aside.

In a heavy medium-size saucepan, melt the butter and heat the olive oil over medium heat. Add the onion and garlic and cook for about 2 minutes, stirring occasionally, until they're softened but not brown. Add the lamb or beef and cook for another 3 minutes, stirring frequently. Stir in the tomato paste, then add the cauliflower florets, green peppers, tomatoes, Turkish red pepper, dill, parsley, and stock. Season with salt and pepper.

Bring the mixture to a boil, then lower the heat, cover the saucepan and simmer for 45 minutes. Remove the saucepan from the heat and stir in the lemon juice. Serve warm.

~ Chicken Breasts Stuffed with Rice, Pistachios, and Herbs

½ pound okra, trimmed
2 medium tomatoes, peeled and cut in thick slices
½ cup chicken stock (page 58)

Heat the oven to 350°F.

Melt the butter in a large skillet over medium heat and gently cook the chicken, stirring, for about 3 minutes, until it's lightly browned all over. Using a slotted spoon, remove the chicken from the skillet and set it aside.

Heat the olive oil in the skillet over high heat and gently fry the eggplant slices on both sides until they're lightly browned, about 2 minutes. Using a slotted spoon, transfer the eggplant to paper towels to absorb the excess oil. Add the zucchini then the green peppers to the skillet and fry them gently to brown them all over.

Place a layer of eggplant slices inside an earthenware or clay pot and lay the zucchini, green peppers, and beans over the eggplant slices. Sprinkle on the dill and parsley. Season with salt and pepper. Pare around the cone-shaped tops of the okra, then layer the okra, then the tomatoes, on top. Cover the layered vegetables with the chicken strips, then pour over the stock. Cover the pot and bake the mixture for about 35 minutes, or until the vegetables are tender and the chicken is cooked through. Serve warm.

SEAFOOD

~ ~

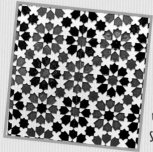

FRESH FISH IS PLENTIFUL EVERYWHERE in Turkey, but naturally it's a specialty of coastal areas. Local people will tell you where and when the fish was caught, assuring you of its freshness. Some of the most delicious fish dishes are also the most simple, such as skewered swordfish chunks char-grilled with chunks of green pepper, tomato, and onion and flavored with bay leaves (page 110).

Seafood stews are made with whatever happens to be plentiful—large shrimp, squid, and chunks of firm white fish. Usually they are cooked in a clay pot, with the fish simmered in a light tomato sauce.

Sometimes fish is simply grilled. An exotic way of preparing it is to flavor it with *rakı*—the anise-flavored liqueur—and roll it in parchment paper (page 106). One of the most dramatic Turkish dishes is Char-Grilled Sardines in Grape Leaves (page 98).

Turkish cooks take full advantage of the many types of fish available, and these recipes reflect that. However, in most cases, similar fish may be substituted. Any recipe calling for gray mullet, for example, can be made with another full-flavored fish, such as bluefish or sea bass; red snapper can be substituted for red mullet, and smelts can be used in place of fresh sardines.

~~~~~~~~~~~~~~~~~

Asma Yaprağında
Sardalye Izgarası

Char-Grilled Sardines in Grape Leaves

SERVES 4

This unusual way of grilling small fish is a specialty of the Mediterranean and western regions of Turkey. In some towns along the Aegean Sea, cooks wrap small fish in tender fig leaves and grill them. You can substitute red mullet or smelt for the sardines.

16 large grape leaves
16 large fresh sardines (total weight about 2 1/2 pounds)
Salt and freshly ground black pepper
1 small Spanish onion, grated (1/2 cup)
1 1/2 teaspoons ground cumin
1/3 cup virgin olive oil
1/4 cup lemon juice
1 lemon

Carefully separate the grape leaves. Cut off the small protruding stems and soak the leaves in warm water for about 10 minutes. Rinse them under cold running water and drape them over the edge of a colander, overlapping as little as possible. Let them drain and set them aside.

Scale and clean the fish. Carefully remove the bones. Wash the fish under running cold water and pat them dry with paper towels. Sprinkle each one with salt and pepper. Rub the inside of the fish with the grated onion and sprinkle on the cumin.

Whisk together the olive oil and lemon juice. Season with salt and pepper. Place the fish in a shallow nonreactive dish and pour this marinade over the fish, turning the fish to coat thoroughly. Cover the dish and refrigerate for 20 minutes.

Prepare a charcoal grill, with the rack set 4 to 5 inches above the coals.

Place the grape leaves shiny side down on a work surface. Brush them with a little of the marinade. Wrap each fish carefully in a grape leaf. Place the wrapped fish seam side down on the grill for about 8 minutes, turning frequently and gently brushing the fish with marinade from the dish.

Open the grape leaves. Squeeze lemon over the sardines and serve. (In this dish, the grape leaves are not eaten.)

~~~~~~~~~~~~~~~~~~~~

Izgara Dil Balığı Şiş Kebabı

Char-Grilled Fillet of Sole Shish Kebab

SERVES 4

This unusual way of grilling flat fish (like sole or flounder) keeps it from falling apart and gives it a wonderful flavor. Use only fresh, firm fish. You will cook the skewered fish and vegetables directly over the charcoals, so you will need 4 skewers, 15 inches long, or long enough to extend across the width of your grill, for this recipe.

1/2 cup virgin olive oil
1/4 cup lemon juice
Salt and freshly ground black pepper
8 skinless sole or flounder fillets (total weight about 2 pounds) cut in half lengthwise
1 large Spanish onion, cut in quarters (1 cup)
3 small Italian green peppers, quartered, seeded, and each cut into 4 pieces crosswise
3 medium tomatoes, quartered and seeded
12 fresh or dried bay leaves
2 tablespoons chopped fresh Italian parsley

In a bowl whisk together the olive oil and lemon juice. Season with salt and pepper. Place the fish in a nonreactive dish and pour over the marinade, turning the fish to coat thoroughly. Cover the dish and refrigerate for about 20 minutes.

Prepare a charcoal grill. Remove the rack, as the fish is cooked directly over the coals.

Starting from the tail end, roll up each fillet of sole.

Prepare the kebabs. On 4 skewers, beginning with a layer of onion, green pepper, tomato, and bay leaves, alternate the rolled sole with the vegetables. You should have 2 rolled fillets per skewer.

Grill the skewers for about 10 minutes, turning frequently and gently brushing the fish and vegetables with the marinade from the dish. Garnish with chopped parsley and serve at once.

~~~~~~~~~~~~~~~~~~~~

Dil Balığı Sarması

Sole Stuffed with Pine Nuts and Spinach

SERVES 6

1/4 cup virgin olive oil
1/4 cup pine nuts
1/2 bunch scallions, finely chopped, white parts only (1/4 cup)
12 ounces chopped fresh spinach leaves
4 garlic cloves, minced
12 skinless sole or flounder fillets (total weight about 3 pounds)
Salt and freshly ground black pepper
3 tablespoons unsalted butter
2 teaspoons paprika
1 1/2 teaspoons Turkish red pepper or ground pepper
1 large tomato, peeled, seeded, and finely chopped (3/4 cup)
3/4 cup dry white wine
2 tablespoons lemon juice
1 tablespoon finely chopped fresh dill
1/4 cup chopped fresh Italian parsley

Heat the olive oil in a large skillet over medium heat, then stir in the pine nuts and cook for about 4 minutes, until they're golden brown. Stir in the scallions, spinach, and garlic. Lower the heat, cover the skillet, and cook the mixture for about 4 minutes, or until the scallions and spinach are wilted. Remove the mixture from the heat and let cool.

Season each fish fillet with salt and pepper. Evenly distribute the spinach mixture among each fillet, placing the mixture in the center and folding over the ends of the fillets to enclose it. Set them aside.

In the same skillet, over medium heat, melt the butter and stir in the paprika, Turkish red pepper, tomato, white wine, and lemon juice. Season with salt and pepper. Add the stuffed fish to the skillet. Sprinkle them with the chopped dill. Lower the heat, cover the skillet, and simmer for about 8 minutes, or until the fish is cooked through. Carefully place the fish on warmed plates, and spoon on the sauce around the fish. Sprinkle with parsley and serve.

~ Overleaf: Char-Grilled Sardines in Grape Leaves

~~~~~~~~~~~~~~~~~~

Pazı Yaprağında Dil Balığı

Fillet of Sole in Swiss Chard Leaves

SERVES 4

4 large Swiss chard leaves
1/4 cup virgin olive oil
3 garlic cloves, minced
4 shallots, finely chopped (1/4 cup)
2 medium tomatoes, peeled, seeded, and finely
   chopped (1 cup)
1/4 cup coarsely chopped fresh Italian parsley,
   plus extra for garnish
Salt and freshly ground black pepper
8 skinless sole or flounder fillets (total weight
   about 2 1/2 pounds)
1/4 cup dry white wine
2 tablespoons lemon juice

Heat the oven to 350°F.

Using a sharp knife, carefully cut off the white stalks from the Swiss chard leaves. In a large pot, bring 4 quarts lightly salted water to a boil. Blanch the Swiss chard leaves for 3 minutes. Using a slotted spoon, remove each leaf from the water and plunge it into cold water to stop it from cooking. Arrange the leaves over the rim of a colander and let them drain well. Cut the Swiss chard leaves in half lengthwise to make a total of 8 leaves.

In a large, heavy saucepan, heat the olive oil. Using a wooden spoon, stir in the garlic and shallots and cook them for about 3 minutes, or until they're softened but not brown. Add the tomatoes and parsley. Season with salt and pepper. Cook gently for about 10 minutes, stirring occasionally. Remove the mixture from the heat and set it aside.

Place a fillet on each of the Swiss chard leaves. Carefully wrap the Swiss chard around the fish, and place the packets side by side, seam side down, in an ovenproof dish. Pour the tomato mixture over the fish, then add the wine and lemon juice. Cover the dish and cook in the oven for about 15 minutes.

Arrange the fish, still wrapped in the leaves, on warmed plates and surround each piece with the sauce. Sprinkle with parsley and serve.

~~~~~~~~~~~~~~~~~~

Kefal Pilakisi

Gray Mullet with Vegetables and Olive Oil

SERVES 4

This method of cooking something in olive oil and vegetables is called *pilaki*. Food cooked this way is often served warm or cool. Gray mullet is a very tasty fish that is abundant in Turkey. Sea bass or bluefish may be substituted if you can't obtain it. This dish is traditionally prepared using whole fish cut up crosswise. You may substitute fillets if you prefer.

2 pounds whole gray mullet
1/2 cup virgin olive oil
2 small Spanish onions, thinly sliced (1 cup)
4 garlic cloves, finely chopped
2 small carrots, thinly sliced (3/4 cup)
1 celery rib, diced (1/2 cup)
2 large tomatoes, peeled and finely sliced (1 1/2 cups)
1 cup coarsely chopped fresh Italian parsley
2 tablespoons finely chopped fresh dill
4 fresh or dried bay leaves
1/2 cup dry white wine
1 tablespoon tomato paste
Salt and freshly ground black pepper
1 lemon, sliced

Scale the fish. To clean them, slit each one along its stomach and carefully remove the intestines and the head. Wash the fish under cold running water and pat them dry with paper towels. Cut them up crosswise into 1-inch-thick pieces.

In a large heavy skillet, heat the oil over medium heat and cook the onion and garlic gently, stirring with a wooden spoon, for about 5 minutes, until they're softened but not brown. Add the carrots, celery, tomatoes, parsley, dill, bay leaves, and white wine. Mix the tomato paste with 1/2 cup water and add this mixture to the skillet. Lower the heat, cover the skillet, and cook for about 10 minutes.

Add the fish to the skillet and season with salt and pepper. Cover the skillet and cook for another 20 minutes, or until the fish and vegetables are tender. Let the fish cool, garnish the fillets with lemon slices, and serve warm or at room temperature.

~~~~~~~~~~~~~~~~~~~

Barbunya Balığı Tavası Zeytinyağlı Limon Soslu

Pan-Fried Red Mullet with Olive Oil Lemon Sauce

SERVES 4

Red mullet is also plentiful in the Mediterranean and Aegean coastal regions of Turkey. One of the more popular ways of serving this delicately flavored fish is with a simple fresh lemon sauce and a salad made with arugula. If you can't obtain red mullet you may use red snapper instead.

OLIVE OIL LEMON SAUCE
>   3 tablespoons extra-virgin olive oil
>   2 tablespoons lemon juice
>   2 tablespoons finely chopped fresh parsley
>   Salt and freshly ground black pepper

>   3 pounds whole red mullets (about 9–12 fish)
>   Salt and freshly ground black pepper
>   3/4 cup all-purpose flour
>   1/2 cup light olive oil or vegetable oil
>   1 sliced lemon

To make the sauce, whisk together the olive oil, lemon juice, and chopped parsley in a small bowl. Season with salt and pepper. Refrigerate.

Scale the fish. To clean it, slit the fish along its stomach and carefully remove the intestines, then remove the gills from the head. Leave the head attached. Wash the fish under cold running water. Pat it dry with paper towels. Season the fish with salt and pepper and coat them lightly all over with the flour.

In a large skillet, heat the olive oil for frying over high heat. When the oil's hot, lower the heat to medium and fry the fish for about 3 minutes on each side, until they're cooked through. Do not crowd them in the pan, and cook them in two batches if necessary. Gently shake the pan from time to time so that the fish does not stick.

Arrange the fish on a warmed serving platter and pour over the lemon sauce. Decorate with sliced lemon and serve.

Yeşil Zeytinli ve Kişnişli Barbunya Balığı Tavası

Red Mullet with Green Olives and Fresh Coriander

SERVES 4

On the Mediterranean and Aegean coasts of Turkey, cooks buy their fish the same day they intend to serve it and expect it to be very fresh. Red mullets that live in the stony depths off the coast have dark red skin and are the most popular and most expensive fish. They have a better flavor than red mullets that live in shallow, sandy waters and have a lighter, pinkish skin color.

Red mullet is sold in specialty fish stores. If you can't obtain it, you may use red snapper instead. This recipe is my own creation.

2 pounds red mullet fillets
Salt and freshly ground black pepper
1/2 cup all-purpose flour
1/2 cup virgin olive oil, divided
1/4 cup finely diced red onion
1 small Italian green pepper, seeded and finely
    chopped (1/4 cup)
1/4 cup pitted and chopped green olives
2 medium tomatoes, peeled, seeded, and finely
    chopped (1 cup)
2 tablespoons coarsely chopped fresh coriander leaves
3/4 cup dry white wine
2 tablespoons lemon juice
1/4 cup chopped fresh Italian parsley, for garnish

Season the fish fillets with salt and pepper and lightly coat them with the flour.

In a large skillet, heat 2 tablespoons of the oil over high heat. When the oil's hot, lower the heat to medium. Arrange the fish fillets skin side down in the skillet and cook gently for about 2 or 3 minutes on each side, until they're cooked through. Gently shake the skillet from time to time so that the fish does not stick. Remove the skillet from the heat, transfer the fish to a serving platter, and keep it warm.

Pour off any excess oil from the skillet and heat the remaining oil over medium heat. Stir in the red onion and cook for 1 minute, until it's softened but not brown. Stir in the green pepper, green olives, tomatoes, coriander, white wine, and lemon juice. Season with salt and pepper. Gently cook the sauce for about 3 minutes.

Pour the sauce over the fish fillets, sprinkle with parsley, and serve.

~ Red Mullet with Green Olives and Fresh Coriander

~~~~~~~~~~~~~~

Kağıtta Levrek Buğulama

Sea Bass Poached with Herbs and Rakı in Parchment

SERVES 4

The rakı, an anise-flavored liqueur, makes this popular recipe delicious. When you open the parchment, the wonderfully fragrant steam is released.

1 bunch scallions, finely chopped,
    white parts only (1/2 cup)
1/2 cup finely chopped fresh
    Italian parsley
1 tablespoon finely chopped fresh dill
2 teaspoons finely chopped fresh mint
2 teaspoons paprika
1 teaspoon Turkish red pepper or
    ground red pepper
Salt and freshly ground black pepper
2 tablespoons unsalted clarified butter
    (page 7)
4 sea bass fillets (total weight about
    2 pounds)
4 fresh or dried bay leaves
2 large tomatoes, peeled, seeded,
    and thinly sliced (1 1/2 cups)
2 small Italian green peppers, seeded
    and thinly sliced (3/4 cup)
1/4 cup lemon juice, plus 4 thin
    lemon slices
1/4 cup virgin olive oil
1/4 cup rakı (anise-flavored liqueur)
    or ouzo

Heat the oven to 400°F.

Cut 4 pieces of parchment paper into rectangles large enough to enclose a fillet of fish.

In a bowl, mix the scallions, parsley, dill, mint, paprika, and Turkish red pepper. Season with salt and pepper.

Heat the clarified butter. Brush each piece of parchment with the butter and place a fillet in the center of each sheet lengthwise. Place a bay leaf on top of each fillet. Evenly distribute the scallion-and-herb mixture among the parcels. Place the tomatoes, green peppers, and sliced lemon on top. Sprinkle each parcel with 1 tablespoon each of the lemon juice, olive oil, rakı, and water. Season with salt and pepper.

Make an envelope out of the parchment by bringing the top and bottom edges of the parchment together in the center over the fillet, and folding them down together (as if you were folding down the top of a lunchbag) to enclose the fish tightly. Twist both ends like a candy wrapper and fold them under the fillet. Moisten the tops of the packages with a little water to help make a tight seal. Place the packages on a baking tray and bake them for about 25 minutes.

To serve, open the packages halfway (be careful of the steam) and place one package on each plate.

~ Sea Bass Poached with Herbs and Rakı in
  Parchment

~~~~~~~~~~~~

Deniz Mahsülleri Güveci

Fish and Shellfish Baked in a Clay Pot

SERVES 4–6

This dish is served in individual clay dishes. If you can't obtain them, use small crocks such as those used for French onion soup. When buying mussels, make sure the shells are tightly closed and discard any whose shells are open.

1 pound squid, cleaned and cut into
    1-inch-thick rings
12 medium-size shrimp, peeled and
    deveined
18 mussels in their shells (about 1 pound),
    scrubbed and beards removed
1/3 cup finely chopped shallots
2 garlic cloves, minced
2 fresh or dried bay leaves
1/3 cup finely chopped fresh Italian parsley,
    plus extra for garnish
3 medium Italian green peppers, seeded and
    thinly sliced (1 cup)
4 large tomatoes, peeled, seeded, and
    chopped (2 1/2 cups)
3/4 cup white wine
1/2 cup virgin olive oil
1 pound swordfish, cut into 1-inch cubes
1 pound flounder or sole, cut into
    1 1/2-inch chunks
1/2 teaspoon Turkish red pepper or ground red pepper
1 teaspoon fresh oregano
Salt and freshly ground black pepper
3 tablespoons all-purpose flour
2 ounces crumbled feta cheese (1/4 cup)

To clean the squid, wash it in cold water, remove the tentacles and the head, peel back and remove the skin from the hood, and rinse it again in cold water. Cut the white flesh into 1-inch rings and set them aside.

To clean the shrimp, remove the head and peel off the legs and hard shell. Using the tip of a small, sharp knife, devein the shrimp (remove the dark line just below the surface of the back). Rinse the shrimp and set them aside.

Heat the oven to 350°F.

Place the mussels in a large nonreactive pot. Add the shallots, garlic, bay leaves, parsley, green peppers, tomatoes, and white wine. Cover the pot and place it over high heat for about 6 minutes, until the mussels open, stirring occasionally to bring the mussels on the bottom of the pan to the top. Remove the mussels from the steaming broth with a skimmer. Discard the bay leaves, and keep the broth warm. When they're cool enough to handle, remove the mussels from their shells and set them aside.

In a heavy, large skillet over medium heat, heat the oil. Stir in the swordfish, flounder, squid, shrimp, and steamed mussels. Add the Turkish red pepper and oregano. Season with salt and pepper. Sprinkle the seafood with the flour and add the warm mussel broth. Stir everything together gently with a wooden spoon, trying not to break up the pieces of fish. Remove the pot from the heat.

Divide the seafood and broth between 4–6 individual clay pots. Bake them for about 15 minutes, or until the fish is cooked through. Top each pot with crumbled feta cheese and cook under the broiler about 2 minutes, until the cheese has melted and is golden brown. Garnish with parsley and serve.

~ Fish and Shellfish Baked in a Clay Pot

~~~~~~~~~~~~~~~~

Halikarnas Karides Güveci

Shrimp Baked in a Clay Pot

SERVES 4

This recipe is named after the Turkish author Cevat Şakir Kabaağaçlı who is known as the Fisherman of Halicarnassus.

 24 large shrimp, peeled and deveined
   (a little over a pound)
 4 tablespoons virgin olive oil
 1/3 cup finely chopped shallots
 4 garlic cloves, minced
 2 medium Italian green peppers, seeded and thinly
   sliced (3/4 cup)
 1/3 cup scallions, finely chopped, white parts only
 1 teaspoon finely chopped fresh oregano
 1/2 tablespoon finely chopped fresh dill
 2 fresh or dried bay leaves
 1 tablespoon paprika
 1 teaspoon Turkish red pepper or ground red pepper
 2 large tomatoes, peeled, seeded, and finely chopped
   (1 1/2 cups)
 1/3 cup finely chopped fresh Italian parsley, plus
   extra for garnish
 3/4 cup dry white wine
 Salt and freshly ground black pepper
 2 ounces crumbled feta cheese (1/4 cup)

To clean the shrimp, remove the heads, then peel off the legs and hard shells. Using the tip of a small, sharp knife, devein the shrimp (remove the dark line just below the surface of the back). Rinse the shrimp and set them aside.

Heat the oven to 350°F.

In a large heavy skillet heat the oil over medium heat. Stir in the shallots and garlic and cook them for about 3 minutes, stirring frequently, or until they're softened but not brown. Add the green peppers and scallions and cook for another 2 minutes, to soften the green peppers. Add the shrimp, oregano, dill, bay leaves, paprika, Turkish red pepper, tomatoes, parsley, and wine. Season with salt and pepper. Cook gently for about 10 minutes, stirring occasionally.

Divide the shrimp and sauce between 4 individual clay pots.

Bake them for about 10 minutes, or until the mixture is heated through. Then top each pot with the crumbled feta cheese and cook under the broiler for about 2 minutes, until the cheese has melted and is golden brown. Sprinkle with parsley and serve.

~~~~~~~~~~~~~~~~

Izgara Kılıç Şiş Kebabı

Char-Grilled Swordfish Shish Kebab

SERVES 4

This is a simple and delicious recipe for cooking swordfish; the tangy marinade makes it melt in your mouth. Don't overcook the fish—it should be cooked until it is slightly rare to medium. Serve it with Olive Oil and Lemon Sauce (page 12) and Shepherd's Salad (page 127).

MARINADE
 1 small Spanish onion, grated (1/2 cup)
 3 garlic cloves, minced
 1/3 cup lemon juice
 2 teaspoons paprika
 1/2 cup virgin olive oil
 4 fresh or dried bay leaves, crumbled
 Salt and freshly ground black pepper

 2 pounds swordfish, cut into 1-inch cubes
 2 tablespoons coarsely chopped fresh Italian parsley

In a bowl whisk together the marinade ingredients. Season with salt and pepper. Place the swordfish in a nonreactive dish and pour over the marinade, turning the fish to coat it thoroughly. Cover the dish and refrigerate for about 2 hours.

Prepare a charcoal grill, with the rack set 4–5 inches above the coals.

Arrange the swordfish cubes on 4 skewers. Grill them for about 8 minutes, turning frequently and gently brushing the fish with marinade from the dish. Pull out the swordfish from the skewers, sprinkle with parsley, and serve at once.

VARIATION: Alternate the swordfish cubes on a skewer with quartered onion; quartered, seeded green peppers; quartered, seeded tomatoes; and fresh bay leaves (or dried if fresh are unavailable).

~ Char-Grilled Swordfish Shish Kebab

PILAFS

~ ~

RICE IS USED EXTENSIVELY IN TURKISH cuisine. It is featured in many of the stuffed meat and vegetable dishes as well as being served as pilaf, and Turkish cooks have very high standards for its preparation. Pilafs are those exotic rice dishes flavored with spices, nuts, and fruits—others, made with meat, fish, and vegetables, are known as *sultan pilavı* (one variation appears on page 120). Pilafs are usually served as an accompaniment to a main course of meat or fish, but some more substantial pilafs, like Yufkalı Pilav (page 117) and Safranlı Midyeli Pilav (page 118) can be served with a salad to make a full meal. İç Pilavı (page 120), with currants, pine nuts, and calves' liver, is served all over Turkey, especially on special occasions. Acılı Bulgur Pilavı (page 120) is actually made with bulgur, or cracked wheat, which has a nutty flavor. In the summer, some pilafs are served cold with plain yogurt.

The preparation of pilaf is as much an art today as it was in the sultan's kitchen, and every good pilaf starts with good rice. First the rice is rinsed well in several washings; then it is soaked for about 30 minutes and drained. This process makes the rice fluffy, and prevents the grains from sticking together.

Method for Preparing Rice
Place the rice in a bowl and cover it with about 4 inches of warm water. Stir the rice for a few seconds, then drain it. Repeat this process several times. Then cover the rice with hot water and set aside for about 30 minutes. Drain the rice well, and let it stand for 10 minutes before cooking.

~~~~~~~~~~~~~~~~~

Nohutlu Pilav

Rice Pilaf with Chickpeas

SERVES 4–6

1½ cups cooked chickpeas (¾ cup uncooked)
4 tablespoons unsalted clarified butter (page 7)
1 small Spanish onion, diced (½ cup)
1½ cup long-grain white rice, washed, soaked,
    and drained (page 112)
2 medium tomatoes, peeled, seeded,
    and finely chopped (1 cup)
2⅓ cups chicken stock (page 58) or water
Salt and freshly ground black pepper

To cook dried chickpeas, soak them overnight (see page 7). Drain them and bring them to a boil in 1½ cups water with 1 teaspoon salt. Lower the heat, simmer 1 hour until just tender, and drain them.

In a heavy, medium-size saucepan, heat the butter over medium heat and cook the onion gently for about 2 minutes, stirring with a wooden spoon. Add the rice and continue stirring for about 2 minutes until the rice is coated with butter. Add the tomatoes and stir for 1 more minute. Pour in the stock. Season with salt and pepper. Bring the mixture to a boil, lower the heat, cover the pan, and cook gently for 10 minutes, until the rice has absorbed all the liquid. Stir in the chickpeas about 5 minutes before the end of cooking. Let the pilaf stand for about 5 minutes, then serve.

~~~~~~~~~~~~~~~~~

Peyaz Pilav

White Rice Pilaf

SERVES 4–6

This is a simple, everyday pilaf that can be served with grilled kebabs or lamb stewed with vegetables.

4 tablespoons unsalted clarified butter (page 7)
1½ cups long-grain white rice, washed, soaked,
    and drained (page 112)
2½ cups hot chicken stock (page 58) or water
Salt and freshly ground black pepper

~ Rice Pilaf with Chicken, Almonds, and Pistachios

Heat the butter in a heavy saucepan set over medium heat. Add the rice and stir with a wooden spoon for 2 minutes, until the rice is coated with butter. Pour in the chicken stock and season with salt and pepper. Bring the liquid to a boil, then lower the heat, cover the saucepan, and cook gently for about 15 minutes, until the rice has absorbed all the liquid.

Remove the saucepan from the heat, and let the pilaf stand, covered, for 5 minutes; then stir the rice and serve.

~~~~~~~~~~~~~~~~~

İstanbul Pilavı

**Rice Pilaf with Chicken, Almonds,
and Pistachios**

SERVES 4–6

4 tablespoons unsalted clarified butter (page 7)
⅓ cup blanched and chopped almonds
⅓ cup blanched and chopped pistachios
1 pound boneless and skinless chicken breasts,
    cut into ½-inch cubes
2½ cups chicken stock (page 58) or water, divided
Salt and freshly ground black pepper
1½ cups long-grain white rice, washed, soaked,
    and drained (page 112)
¼ teaspoon saffron threads, crumbled and soaked
    in ¼ cup warm water
1 tablespoon finely chopped fresh dill

In a large, heavy skillet, heat 2 tablespoons butter over medium heat and lightly brown the almonds and pistachios for about 2 minutes. Stir in the chicken pieces. Lower the heat, then add ¼ cup of the stock. Season with salt and pepper. Cook the chicken for about 3 minutes, stirring occasionally, until the chicken is lightly cooked all over. Remove the skillet from the heat and set it aside.

In a heavy medium-size saucepan, heat the remaining butter and stir in the rice, coating it all over with the butter. Add the soaked saffron with water. Season with salt and pepper. Pour in the remaining stock. Bring the mixture to a boil, then lower the heat, cover the saucepan, and cook gently for about 10 minutes.

Gently stir in the reserved chicken mixture and cook for another 8 minutes, or until the rice has absorbed all of the liquid. Remove the saucepan from the heat and stir in the dill. Let the pilaf stand, covered, for about 5 minutes, then serve.

~~~~~~~~~~~~~~~~~

Yufkalı Pilav

Rice Pilaf with Vegetables in Pastry

SERVES 6

This is an elegant way of serving rice for any occasion. It makes a light meal accompanied by a salad.

2½ cups chicken stock (page 58) or water
1 carrot, finely diced (½ cup)
½ cup fresh or frozen peas (if using frozen, soak them in warm water before you use them)
1 rib celery, finely diced (⅓ cup)
Salt
8 tablespoons unsalted clarified butter (page 7), divided
1 small Spanish onion, finely diced (½ cup) ·
1½ cups long-grain white rice, rinsed, soaked, and drained (page 112)
2 pounds boneless and skinless chicken breasts, cut into 1-inch cubes
Freshly ground black pepper
¼ cup finely chopped fresh dill
3 tablespoons finely chopped fresh Italian parsley
¼ cup milk
2 egg yolks
10 sheets filo dough

Heat the oven to 400°F.

In a saucepan over medium heat, combine the stock, carrots, peas, and celery. Season with salt. Bring the mixture to a boil, then lower the heat and simmer for about 10 minutes. Strain the stock and reserve it. Set the vegetables aside.

In a heavy, medium saucepan over medium heat, heat 3 tablespoons of the butter and cook the onion for about 2 minutes, stirring with a wooden spoon, until it's softened but not brown. Add the rice and cook, stirring constantly, until the rice is coated with butter. Add the reserved vegetables and chicken and pour in the reserved stock. Season with salt and freshly ground black pepper.

Bring the mixture to a boil, then lower the heat, cover the saucepan, and cook gently for about 15 minutes, until the rice has absorbed the liquid. Remove the saucepan from the heat and gently stir in the dill and parsley. Cover the saucepan and set the pilaf aside.

Mix the remaining butter with the milk and egg yolks in a bowl. Brush the inside of a round 12 x 2-inch casserole dish with this mixture. Line the casserole dish with 1 sheet of filo dough, letting one end of dough hang over the rim of the dish. Brush the dough lightly with the egg mixture. Lay a second filo dough sheet on top of the first, only this time let one end of dough hang over the end of a different part of the dish's rim. Continue layering the filo dough in this manner, brushing egg mixture between each layer and making sure that the entire rim of the dish has dough hanging over it.

Spoon the cooled rice pilaf into the filo-dough-lined dish. Fold each piece of hanging dough over the rice, pressing down gently. Brush the top with the remaining egg mixture. Bake for about 15 minutes, lower the heat to 350°F, and bake for another 5 minutes, or until the top is golden brown. Let the pilaf stand for about 5 minutes, then cut into slices and serve.

~ Rice Pilaf with Vegetables in Pastry

~~~~~~~~~~~~~~~~~

Müceddere

Rice Pilaf with Chickpeas, Green Lentils, and Caramelized Onions

SERVES 4–6

The onions in this specialty of eastern Turkey make it smell wonderful, and the chickpeas and lentils make it tasty and nutritious. It is also a good vegetarian entrée that can be served cold with plain yogurt.

1/3 cup cooked green lentils (1/4 cup dried)
1/2 cup cooked chickpeas (1/4 cup dried)
4 tablespoons virgin olive oil
3 small Spanish onions, sliced (1 1/2 cups)
2 teaspoons sugar
Salt and freshly ground black pepper
1 tablespoon lemon juice
1/2 cup long-grain white rice, washed, soaked, and drained (page 112)
1/4 cup orzo
2 medium tomatoes, peeled, seeded, and chopped (1 cup)
1 tablespoon ground cumin
1 teaspoon Turkish red pepper or ground red pepper
2 cups chicken stock (page 58) or water
1/4 cup coarsely chopped fresh Italian parsley

Soak the dried chickpeas overnight (page 7). The next day, drain them and in a small pan bring them to a boil in I cup water with 1/2 teaspoon salt. Lower the heat and simmer 45 minutes, until just tender. At the same time, cook the dried lentils in another pan with 2/3 cup water. Bring to a boil, then simmer until just tender, about 15 to 20 minutes.

In a heavy, medium-size saucepan, heat the oil over medium heat. Add the onions and sugar, and season with salt and pepper. Cover the saucepan and cook gently for 5 minutes, or until the onions are tender. Uncover the pan, increase the heat to high, and stir in the lemon juice. Cook, stirring, until the onions are browned.

Add the rice and orzo, and cook, stirring, for 2 minutes. Add the tomatoes, lentils, chickpeas, cumin, and Turkish red pepper. Pour in the stock. Lower the heat, cover the saucepan, and cook gently for about 20 minutes, or until all the liquid has been absorbed. Stir in the parsley and let the pilaf stand, covered, in a warm place for 5 minutes; then serve.

~~~~~~~~~~~~~~~~~

Safranlı Midyeli Pilav

Rice Pilaf with Saffron and Mussels

SERVES 4–6

This is an unusual way to prepare mussels. The saffron makes the rice bright yellow, and the mussels contrast nicely with it. When buying mussels, make sure the shells are tightly closed and discard any whose shells are open.

1 1/2 pounds mussels (about 27 mussels), cleaned and beards removed
2 1/2 cups chicken stock (page 58) or water
1/4 cup virgin olive oil
1 small Spanish onion, diced (1/2 cup)
1 1/2 cups white long-grain rice, washed, soaked, and drained (page 112)
2 medium tomatoes, peeled, seeded, and finely chopped (1 cup)
1/4 teaspoon saffron threads, crumbled and soaked in 1/4 cup warm water
Salt and freshly ground black pepper
3 tablespoons finely chopped fresh dill

Place the mussels in a large nonreactive pan and add the stock. Cover the pan and bring the liquid to a boil for about 5 minutes, stirring occasionally, until the mussels open. Using a skimmer, remove the mussels from the pan. When they're cool enough to handle, remove the mussels from their shells and set them aside. Strain the stock and reserve it.

In a heavy, medium-size saucepan, heat the olive oil over medium heat and cook the onion gently for about 2 minutes, stirring with a wooden spoon, until it's softened but not brown. Add the rice and continue cooking, stirring, until the rice is coated with oil. Add the tomatoes and saffron with water.

Pour in the reserved stock and season with salt and pepper. Bring the mixture to a boil, then lower the heat, cover the saucepan, and cook gently for about 10 minutes. Gently stir in the reserved mussels and cook for another 5 minutes, or until the rice has absorbed all the liquid. Remove the saucepan from the heat. Stir in the dill. Let the pilaf stand for about 5 minutes, then serve.

~ Rice Pilaf with Saffron and Mussels

~~~~~~~~~~~~~~~~~~

Acılı Bulgur Pilavı

Bulgur Pilaf with Peppers and Tomatoes

SERVES 4–6

4 tablespoons unsalted clarified butter (page 7)
1 large Spanish onion, diced (1 cup)
1 small Italian green pepper, finely chopped (1/4 cup)
1 1/2 cups coarse-grain bulgur, washed and drained
3 medium tomatoes, peeled, seeded, and
    finely chopped (2 cups)
2 1/2 teaspoons Turkish red pepper or ground red
    pepper
2 1/2 cups chicken stock (page 58) or hot water
Salt and freshly ground black pepper
2 tablespoons coarsely chopped fresh Italian parsley

In a heavy, medium-size saucepan, heat the butter over medium heat and cook the onion gently for 2 minutes, stirring with a wooden spoon, until it's softened but not brown. Stir in the green pepper, bulgur, tomatoes, Turkish red pepper, and stock. Season with salt and pepper. Bring the mixture to a boil, then lower the heat, cover the saucepan, and cook gently for about 15 minutes, or until the bulgur has absorbed all the liquid. Let the mixture stand, covered, for about 5 minutes; then stir in the parsley, and serve.

~~~~~~~~~~~~~~~~~~

İç Pilavı

Rice Pilaf with Currants and Pine Nuts

SERVES 4–6

1/4 cup dried black currants
4 tablespoons unsalted clarified butter (page 7)
1/3 cup pine nuts
1 small Spanish onion, diced (1/2 cup)
1/4 pound lamb or calves' liver, cut into 1/2-inch cubes
    (optional)
1 1/2 cups white long-grain rice, washed, soaked,
    and drained (page 112)
1 teaspoon ground cinnamon
1 teaspoon sugar
Salt and freshly ground black pepper
2 1/2 cups chicken stock (page 58) or water
2 tablespoons finely chopped fresh Italian
    parsley leaves
1/4 cup finely chopped fresh dill

Soak the currants in warm water for 20 minutes. Drain them and set them aside.

In a heavy, medium-size saucepan, heat the butter over medium heat and cook the pine nuts and onion gently for about 3 minutes, stirring with a wooden spoon, until both are lightly browned. Stir in the liver, if you're using it, then add the rice, currants, cinnamon, and sugar. Season with salt and pepper. Pour in the stock and bring the mixture to a boil; then lower the heat, cover the saucepan, and cook gently for about 15 minutes until all the liquid has been absorbed and the rice is tender. Stir in the parsley and dill. Let the pilaf stand, covered, for about 5 minutes, then serve.

~~~~~~~~~~~~~~~~~~

Sultan Pilavı

Sultan's Rice Pilaf

SERVES 4–6

This recipe was prepared for the sultans in the kitchens of the Topkapı Palace. It can be served as a meal, accompanied by Cucumbers with Yogurt and Mint (page 38).

2 small Italian eggplants, peeled and diced (2 cups)
Salt
6 tablespoons virgin olive oil, divided
3 medium tomatoes, peeled, seeded, and chopped
    (2 cups)
White Rice Pilaf (page 115)
1 tablespoon finely chopped fresh Italian parsley

MEATBALLS
1 slice day-old bread, crusts removed
1/2 pound ground lean lamb or beef
2 eggs
1 teaspoon ground cumin
1 tablespoon finely chopped fresh Italian parsley
1/2 teaspoon Turkish red pepper or ground red pepper
Salt and freshly ground black pepper
1/3 cup all-purpose flour

Place the eggplant in a bowl and sprinkle it with salt; then cover it with cold water and set aside for 20 minutes.

Soak the bread in cold water briefly and squeeze out the excess water. To make the meatball mixture, combine the meat, bread, eggs, cumin, parsley, and Turkish red pepper in a bowl.

Season with salt and pepper. Mix well for about 2 minutes. Cover the bowl and refrigerate for about 15 minutes.

Shape the meat mixture into 24 small meatballs. Dust them with the flour. In a heavy, large skillet, heat 2 tablespoons of the olive oil over high heat and brown the meatballs all over for about 3 minutes. Stir in the tomatoes, cover the skillet, lower the heat, and cook gently for about 12 minutes. Remove the skillet from the heat and let it stand.

Drain and rinse the eggplant and pat it dry with paper towels. In a separate skillet, heat the remaining oil over medium heat and gently fry the diced eggplant until it's brown all over.

Stir the white rice pilaf and place it on individual warmed plates. Make a well in the center of each serving and divide the eggplant among the plates. Top with the meatballs, sprinkle with parsley, and serve at once.

~ Bulgur Pilaf with Peppers and Tomatoes

SALADS

VEGETABLES ARE A VERY important part of the Turkish diet, and fresh salads are an essential part of most meals. They are served with the main course. Most salads are simply made with leafy greens, tomatoes, cucumbers, green peppers, and whatever other vegetables are in season.

Salads made with beans, grains, and vegetables are frequently a part of a winter *meze*. Edible wild greens such as dandelions are often cooked and served cold with a drizzle of extra-virgin olive oil or lemon juice.

One of my favorite summer salads (page 126, left) is made with purslane, which has large, light green, oval leaves and green stems. Purslane grows throughout Turkey in the early summer right through to the end of August.

Wild purslane grows everywhere in the United States (*Portulaca oleracea*). It has small oval leaves with purple veins on purple stems. In Turkey, the wild variety, called *pirpirim*, is also cultivated. You can find wild purslane in specialty markets, and I grow it myself in my home garden. The soft, lemony leaves, tossed with lemon and olive oil and flavored with garlic, make a delicious accompaniment to grilled meat or fish.

Another favorite salad is made with daikon—a large winter radish—which has a mild flavor and is delicious when mixed with grated carrots (page 128).

~~~~~~~~~~~~~~

Hindiba Salatası

Dandelion Salad

SERVES 4–6

This is one of my favorite summer salads. It is easy to prepare and has a slightly bitter flavor. Serve it with grilled meat, fish, or chicken. Dandelion greens are easy to find these days in most well-stocked markets. Look in gourmet markets if your supermarket doesn't have them.

This recipe was served to more than 1500 guests at the James Beard Awards Dinner in May 1995.

2 pounds dandelion greens
1/4 cup lemon juice
1/3 cup extra-virgin olive oil
Salt and freshly ground black pepper
Mixed olives
Lemon wedges

Trim the dandelion greens by cutting off the roots to separate the stems. Remove any brown or wilted leaves and stems. Wash them well.

In a heavy, large saucepan, bring 2 quarts cold water to a boil. Add the dandelion greens and boil them for about 8 minutes, or until they're tender. Drain the greens well and squeeze them to remove the excess water.

Coarsely chop the dandelion greens. Place them in a bowl and add the lemon juice and olive oil. Season with salt and pepper and toss well. Cover the bowl and refrigerate for at least 30 minutes.

Garnish with olives and lemon wedges, and serve chilled.

~~~~~~~~~~~~~~

Kara Lahana Salatası

Collard Green Salad with Yogurt-Garlic Sauce

SERVES 4–6

This salad is a specialty of the Black Sea region of Turkey. Serve it as a light lunch on hot days.

3 tablespoons virgin olive oil or vegetable oil
1 small Spanish onion, finely diced (1/2 cup)
1/2 cup long-grain rice
2 medium tomatoes, peeled and coarsely chopped
    (1 cup)
2 long Italian green peppers, seeded and finely
    chopped (1/2 cup)
2 cups water or chicken stock (page 58)
2 pounds collard greens, coarsely chopped
    (include tender stems)
Salt and freshly ground black pepper
1 recipe Yogurt-Garlic Sauce (page 13)
Paprika

In a large, heavy saucepan, heat the olive oil over medium heat. Add the onion and cook gently for about 2 minutes, or until it's softened but not brown. Stir in the rice, tomatoes, and green peppers. Pour in the water or stock. Add the chopped collard greens and season with salt and pepper. Cover the saucepan, lower the heat, and cook gently for about 20 minutes, or until the collard greens are tender and all the liquid has been absorbed.

Transfer the contents of the saucepan to a serving dish, cover the dish, and refrigerate for about 1 hour. To serve, pour the yogurt-garlic sauce over the salad and sprinkle paprika over the sauce. This dish is best served chilled or at room temperature.

~ *Top to bottom:* Dandelion Salad and Collard Green Salad with Yogurt-Garlic Sauce

~ Bulgur and Walnut Salad

~~~~~~~~~~~~~~~~

Mercimek Piyazı

Green Lentil Salad

SERVES 4–6

1½ cups dried green lentils
1 bunch scallions, trimmed and finely chopped,
    some green parts included (½ cup)
2 medium tomatoes, peeled, seeded, and finely diced
    (1 cup)
2 garlic cloves, chopped
½ cup coarsely chopped fresh Italian parsley leaves
4 sprigs fresh mint leaves, finely chopped
1½ teaspoons ground cumin
½ teaspoon Turkish red pepper or ground red pepper
¼ cup extra-virgin olive oil
2 tablespoons white wine vinegar
2 tablespoons lemon juice
Salt and freshly ground black pepper
Romaine lettuce
Toasted pita bread

Bring the lentils to a boil in a large saucepan with 2½ cups of water. Lower the heat, cover, and simmer for about 35 minutes, or until the lentils are tender. If necessary, add a little extra water to extend cooking time, but do not overcook, or the lentils will disintegrate.

Place the lentils in a large bowl. Add all the remaining ingredients, except the romaine lettuce and the pita bread. Season with salt and pepper and toss well. Cover and chill for at least 15 minutes. Arrange on a bed of romaine lettuce and serve chilled with toasted pita bread.

~~~~~~~~~~~~~~~~

Nohut Piyazı

Chickpea Salad

SERVES 4–6

2 cups dried chickpeas, soaked and drained (page 7),
    or 4 cups canned, drained
1 small red onion, finely diced (½ cup)
2 medium tomatoes, peeled, seeded, and finely diced
    (1 cup)
2 garlic cloves, chopped
½ bunch finely chopped fresh Italian parsley
½ teaspoon Turkish red pepper or ground red pepper
2 teaspoons ground cumin
2 teaspoons paprika
¼ cup lemon juice
5 tablespoons extra-virgin olive oil
Salt and freshly ground black pepper
Romaine lettuce
Toasted pita bread

If you are using dried chickpeas, cook them by placing them in a medium-size saucepan with 3½ cups of water and 2 teaspoons of salt. Bring the chickpeas to a boil, lower the heat, and simmer for about 1½ hours, or until they are tender. Add more water if it is absorbed too quickly. Drain the chickpeas well.

Place the chickpeas in a bowl along with the onion, tomatoes, garlic, and spices. Pour over the lemon juice and olive oil. Season with salt and pepper and toss well. Cover the bowl and refrigerate for at least 30 minutes. Arrange the mixture on a bed of romaine lettuce and serve chilled with toasted pita bread.

~ Green Lentil Salad

DESSERTS, FRUIT COMPOTES, AND DRINKS

~~~~~~~~~~~~~~~~~~~~~~~~~~

BAKLAVA AND KADAYIF, THOSE intensely sweet, nutty, flaky pastries, are the most familiar Middle Eastern desserts to Westerners. Recipes for baklava vary, and the one at Sultan's Kitchen has earned a reputation for its lightness—sweet without being cloying. The most famous baklava is from the southeastern Turkish cities of Gaziantep and Urfa. They prepare it with painstaking care—from rolling the thinnest possible sheets of fresh filo dough to selecting and grinding the nuts.

In most Turkish recipes you can substitute regular butter for clarified butter, but try to use clarified butter for pastries and desserts—they will last longer at room temperature.

Turkish cuisine has many more desserts to offer than baklava. Two delicious cakes are made with cheese. Suzme Yogurt Tatlısı (page 144) is a light dessert made with yogurt. Peynir Tatlısı (also page 144) is made with feta cheese that is soaked to remove the salt.

Delicious creamy puddings often complete Turkish meals, and shops all around Turkey display puddings decorated with fruits and nuts. Puddings are infused with rose water, vanilla, or mastic, a fragrant pine resin. In these recipes I've thickened them using cornstarch, but in Turkey, they use a thickening agent called *sübye*, which is a mixture of white rice cooked with milk that is ground while still warm. You can use rice flour instead of cornstarch if you prefer.

With all the fruit that is grown during the long sunny months in Turkey, it is not surprising that figs, melons, and sultana grapes as well as citrus fruits have been a part of the cuisine since antiquity. Simple spiced fruit compotes are a typical ending to a large meal, and many homes have large jars of preserved fruits in their larders. Raisin compote is served with the main course, and spoonfuls are eaten with pilaf.

There are many drinks that are uniquely Turkish. Ayran (page 151) is a yogurt-based drink that provides a soothing, creamy complement to spicy foods. Fruit drinks, like Vişne Şerbeti (a sour cherry drink on page 152), are also served at meals or as an afternoon thirst quencher.

Most Turks begin their days with a glass of hot tea, but they also enjoy their coffee, which is more akin to espresso in that it is a steaming hot, intensely flavored liquid. A special coffee pot called a *cezve* is used to make coffee, and a *çaydanlık* is used for tea. Both may be purchased in Middle Eastern supermarkets and are well worth having on hand to provide an authentic finish to a fine Turkish meal.

~~~~~~~~~~~~~~~~~

Baklava Hamuru

Baklava Dough

MAKES 20 SHEETS OF DOUGH

You can make very good baklava with store-bought filo dough, but homemade dough is moister, and your final pastry will be crispier. Homemade filo sheets are not as thin as the machine-pressed dough, and the dough shrinks a little more in cooking than the premade dough. To roll the dough out thinly, you will need a 3/4-inch-diameter, 30-inch-long *oklava*. A wooden dowel from the hardware store works just as well.

2 cups unbleached all-purpose flour, sifted
2 tablespoons salt
4 eggs, room temperature
1/4 cup virgin olive oil
1 1/2 cups water at room temperature (about 70°F)
1/4 cup cornstarch for dusting

Sift the flour with the salt and place on a work table, preferably one with a wooden top. Make a well in the center of the mixture and add the eggs, olive oil, and water to the well. Mix the ingredients slowly to make a dough. Knead the dough, dusting it and your hands lightly with cornstarch now and then to prevent the dough from sticking.

Knead the dough by pressing down on it with the heels of both your palms and pushing it forward to stretch it, then pulling it back toward you, turning the dough as you work. Lightly dust the dough with cornstarch again and knead it this way for about 2 minutes. Roll the dough into a cylinder, then pick it up at both ends and stretch it until it's about 24 inches long. Cover it with a damp cloth and let it rest for about 15 minutes.

Repeat this process two more times, each time kneading the dough for 2 minutes, stretching the dough, and letting the dough rest covered with a damp cloth for 15 minutes.

Turn out the dough onto a cornstarch-dusted surface. Pulling from both ends, reshape the dough into a 24-inch cylinder. Cut it into 20 equal pieces.

Gently flatten each piece of dough with the heel of your palm. Sprinkle the pieces lightly with cornstarch. Spread out the pieces of dough so that they don't touch one another and cover them with a damp cloth. Let them rest for about 15 minutes.

With a regular rolling pin, roll out each piece of dough into a 6-inch diameter circle, lightly dusting both sides with cornstarch. Stack the pieces into 2 piles of 10 each and let them rest for 30 minutes covered with a damp cloth.

Using an oklava, roll out each piece of dough again by pressing down on the center of the dough with the oklava and pushing it toward the outer edge and then pulling it back toward you, rotating the dough with a quick motion after every few rolls. Roll each circle into a 14 x 20-inch-long paper-thin piece. This dough holds together well, so if you want to stretch the dough further and feel comfortable handling it, you can hold the dough vertically and rotate it while gently pulling at the edges. Stretch it this way until you can almost see through it.

To prevent the dough from drying once you have finished rolling it out or stretching it, sprinkle it lightly with cornstarch and cover it with a damp cloth.

Now you are ready to assemble the baklava (page 137).

~~~~~~~~~~~~~~~~

Baklava

MAKES 48 PIECES

My baklava is very light and crispy with a soft, nutty center. Traditionally, it is baked in a round baking pan and is cut into diamond shapes. Cutting the dough halfway down before baking it will allow the top layers of dough to curl under as they cook.

SYRUP

    2¹⁄₂ cups cold water
    3¹⁄₂ cups sugar
    2 tablespoons lemon juice

    3 cups walnuts, plus extra for sprinkling (optional)
    2 tablespoons sugar
    1¹⁄₂ cups unsalted clarified butter (page 7)
    2 packages filo dough, each containing 20 to 22 sheets
       of dough
    Finely chopped pistachio nuts (optional)

Heat the oven to 375°F.

To make the syrup, combine the cold water with the sugar in a medium-size saucepan. Boil the mixture for 5 minutes, then lower the heat and simmer, uncovered, for about 15 minutes. The syrup is ready when it is light yellow, and when a small spoonful dropped onto a wooden surface and cooled is tacky. Stir the lemon juice into the syrup and set it aside to cool.

Place the walnuts and sugar in a food processor. Process until medium to finely ground—do not grind too fine. Set aside.

Brush the inside of a 14 x 18 x 1-inch baking pan all over with a little of the clarified butter. Place 1 sheet of dough in the pan. With a wide pastry brush, lightly brush the dough with a little of the clarified butter. Continue layering the dough and brushing with butter until one package of dough is used.

Spread the walnuts over the dough and lightly sprinkle it with water—using a plant mister is best—to help the dough adhere to the walnuts when the next layer is added. Using the second package of filo dough, layer the dough over the walnuts, brushing each sheet with a little of the butter. Trim the pastry edges to fit neatly in the baking pan. Brush the top layer and the edges with clarified butter.

Using a sharp knife dipped in hot water, cut through the dough halfway down the height of the pan. To make 48 pieces,

make 4 lengthwise cuts and 12 crosswise cuts. (To make triangle-shaped pastries, make 6 cuts crosswise instead of 12, and then cut diagonally across each rectangle. For diamond shapes, cut the dough diagonally in both directions.)

Bake the baklava in the center of the oven for 30 minutes. Lower the heat to 325°F and bake for an additional 30 minutes, until the top is light golden. Remove the baklava from the oven and let it sit at room temperature for about 10 minutes. Recut the pastries along the lines all the way to the bottom of the baking pan and pour the cold syrup evenly over the cut lines. Sprinkle the baklava with ground walnuts or pistachio nuts, if so desired, and let it cool completely. Serve at room temperature.

NOTE: Baklava keeps for one week stored in a cool, dry place.

~~~~~~~~~~~~~~~~~

Yeşil Fıstıklı Revani

Pistachio Semolina Cake

MAKES 16 SLICES

This recipe calls for vanilla crystals, which have a much more intense flavor than vanilla extract. It can be found in specialty shops. If you can't obtain it, use vanilla extract instead.

SYRUP
> 3 1/2 cups cold water
> 3 cups sugar
> 2 tablespoons lemon juice

> 3/4 cup unbleached all-purpose flour, plus extra for dusting
> 8 medium eggs at room temperature, separated
> 1/4 cup sugar
> 1/2 teaspoon vanilla crystals or 1 teaspoon vanilla extract
> 2 teaspoons lemon zest
> Salt
> 1 cup fine-grain semolina
> 1/4 cup finely ground pistachio nuts
> 1 recipe Thick Turkish Cream (page 146) or fresh berries

Heat the oven to 350°F.

To make the syrup, combine the water with the sugar. Boil the mixture for 5 minutes, then lower the heat and simmer, uncovered, for about 15 minutes. Stir the lemon juice into the syrup and let it cool.

Lightly butter and dust with flour the inside of a 10 x 15 x 2-inch baking pan. Place it in the refrigerator until you're ready to use it.

In a large mixing bowl, beat the egg yolks with the sugar, vanilla crystals, and lemon zest until the mixture becomes slightly foamy. Gently fold in the semolina, flour, then the pistachio nuts. Stir the mixture until it's well blended.

Using an electric mixer or a wire whisk, beat the egg whites with a pinch of salt until they form firm peaks, about 3 to 4 minutes. Gently fold the egg whites into the batter. Pour the mixture into the baking pan and spread it out evenly. Bake the cake in the center of the oven for about 35 minutes, until the top is golden brown.

Cut the hot cake into slices and pour the cooled syrup over it. Refrigerate the cake for several hours. Serve it chilled with thick Turkish cream (page 148) or fresh berries.

~ *Clockwise, from the front:* Shredded Filo Dough with Walnuts (page 140), Shredded Filo Dough with Cheese Filling (page 140), Baklava (page 137), and Nightingale's Nests (page 141)

~~~~~~~~~~~~~~~~~~~

Tel Kadayıf

Shredded Filo Dough with Walnuts

MAKES 20 PIECES

This was my favorite dessert when I was growing up. My family had a close friend who supplied us with the shredded dough, called *tel kadayıf*, which can be purchased at Middle Eastern food shops. The crunchy light pastry makes this a lighter alternative to baklava. It can be made with the walnut filling or with the cheese filling of Künefe.

SYRUP

    3 cups cold water
    3 cups sugar
    2 tablespoons lemon juice

    1 pound shredded filo dough
    2 cups walnuts
    1 tablespoon sugar
    3/4 cup unsalted clarified butter (page 7)
    Ground pistachio nuts (optional)
    1 recipe Thick Turkish Cream (page 146) or
        whipped cream

Heat the oven to 375°F.

To make the syrup, combine the water with the sugar. Boil the mixture for 5 minutes, then lower the heat and simmer, uncovered, for about 15 minutes. The syrup is ready when it is light yellow, and when a small spoonful dropped onto a wooden surface and cooled is tacky. Stir the lemon juice into the syrup and let it cool.

Place the walnuts and sugar in a food processor. Process until medium to finely ground—do not grind too fine.

Brush the inside of a 10 x 15 x 2-inch baking pan all over with a little of the clarified butter. Separate the shredded dough in half by holding it upright and pulling it apart. Spread half the dough evenly in the pan. Dip a wide pastry brush into the butter and use it drizzle half the remaining clarified butter over the dough.

Spread the walnuts on the dough, pressing gently. Lightly sprinkle the walnut filling with water—use a plant mister—to help the rest of the dough adhere to it when it is added. Place the other half of the shredded dough over the walnuts and gently press down all over. Drizzle the remaining butter over the dough.

Bake the dessert in the center of the oven for 35 minutes, or until it's light golden. Remove the pastry from the oven and immediately pour over the cooled syrup. Cover the pan and let the pastry cool to room temperature. If you like, sprinkle on ground walnuts or pistachio nuts. Cut the pastry into squares and serve with thick Turkish cream or whipped cream.

~~~~~~~~~~~~~~~~~~~

Künefe

Shredded Filo Dough with Cheese Filling

MAKES 20 PIECES

Use this filling as an alternative to the walnut filling in the Tel Kadaıf. In Turkey, Künefe is made with a thinner dough than the shredded filo dough, and the filling is made with a cheese called *lor*. This cheese is made from the solids of boiled, unpasteurized milk that is left out until it curdles.

NOTE: You will need to soak the feta cheese overnight to remove the salt. This step can be omitted if you use ricotta cheese.

FILLING

    32 ounces (4 cups) quality feta cheese or unsalted
        ricotta cheese
    1/2 cup milk
    1/2 cup heavy cream
    4 tablespoons rose water
    1 cup pistachio nuts, finely ground

Cut the cheese into 1-inch cubes and soak them in a bowl of hot water for about 2 hours, changing the water frequently. Refrigerate the soaking cheese overnight so all of the salt leaches out.

Mix the cheese, milk, and heavy cream together well.

Prepare the dough as for the Tel Kadaıf. Once you have placed half of the shredded filo dough in the baking pan and drizzled it with butter, spread the Künefe over it evenly. Bake as directed for the Tel Kadaıf.

Remove the pastry from the oven, pour the rose water and syrup over it, and sprinkle it with ground pistachio nuts. Serve warm or hot.

~~~~~~~~~~~~~~~~~

Bülbül Yuvası

Nightingale's Nests

MAKES 20–22 PASTRIES

Each of these pastries is a thin sheet of baklava dough that is rolled around a 1/4-inch-diameter oklava, crinkled, and rolled into a coil, to resemble a cinnamon bun. A 1/4-inch dowel, 20 inches long, from the hardware store works just as well if you don't have an oklava—just wash it well before you work with it.

SYRUP
  1 1/2 cups cold water
  2 cups sugar
  1 tablespoon lemon juice

  3 cups walnuts
  1 tablespoon sugar
  1 package filo dough (20 to 22 sheets of dough)
  1 1/4 cup unsalted clarified butter (page 7)
  1/2 cup finely ground pistachio nuts
  1/2 cup finely ground walnuts (optional)

Preheat the oven to 375°F and grease a baking pan.

To make the syrup, combine the cold water with the sugar in a saucepan. Boil the mixture for 3 minutes, then lower the heat and simmer, uncovered, for about 10 minutes. Stir in the lemon juice and let the mixture cool.

Place the walnuts and sugar in a food processor and process until medium to finely ground, but do not grind too finely. Set them aside.

Brush the inside of a 14 x 18 x 1-inch baking pan with enough of the clarified butter to coat it thinly. Place one sheet of filo dough on the work surface so that the shorter end of the dough faces you. Keep the dough that you are not working with covered with a damp cloth to help prevent it from drying out.

Spread 1 1/2 tablespoons of the walnuts in a 1/2-inch strip evenly across the filo dough 1/2 inch in from the end closest to you. Brush the filo with butter.

Press a 1/4-inch-diameter oklava onto the filo dough at the end closest to you and roll the whole filo sheet onto the oklava. Spritz the dough lightly with cold water (use a plant mister) to keep it pliable. Gently push the dough from both ends toward the center of the oklava, wrinkling up the dough until it is about 8 inches long. Gently pull the oklava out of the pastry. Take one end of the pastry "tube" and roll the tube into a flat coil, so that it resembles a cinnamon bun.

Repeat this process with the other pieces of filo, and place the "bird nests" on the greased baking pan.

Bake the pastries for about 25 minutes, or until they are a light golden brown, and remove the pan from the oven. Drain off the excess butter by tilting the pan; discard the excess butter.

Pour the cold syrup over the nests, cover them, and let them sit at room temperature to cool completely. Before serving, sprinkle the middle of each one with ground pistachio nuts and walnuts (if using). Serve cold.

~~~~~~~~~~~~~~~~~~~~~

Tulumba Tatlısı

Fried Pastries in Syrup

MAKES 36 PASTRIES

These delicious pastries are shaped using a piping bag, so they are like golden fingers. They become sweet from soaking up the syrup.

SYRUP

2^1/$_2$ cups sugar

2 cups cold water

1 tablespoon lemon juice

1 cup water at room temperature (about 70°F)

2 tablespoons sugar

1 teaspoon salt

1^1/$_2$ cups unbleached all-purpose flour, sifted

^{1}/$_2$ cup coarse-grained semolina

4 tablespoons unsalted clarified butter (page 7)

^{1}/$_4$ cup cornstarch

3 eggs, room temperature

8 cups light olive oil or vegetable oil

^{1}/$_4$ cup vegetable oil

To make the syrup, combine the 2 cups cold water with the sugar and bring to a boil. Continue boiling for 5 minutes, then lower the heat and simmer uncovered for about 15 minutes. The syrup is ready when it is light yellow, and when a small spoonful dropped onto a wooden surface and cooled is tacky. Stir in the lemon juice and set the syrup aside to cool.

To make the pastry, place 1 cup water, the sugar, and the salt in a saucepan and bring it to a boil. Lower the heat and add the flour and semolina, stirring quickly with a wooden spoon. Cook the flour and the semolina for about 2 minutes.

Transfer the mixture to a large bowl and let it cool for about 20 minutes. When this mixture is cool enough to handle, add the butter and stir. Once it is well mixed, add the cornstarch and blend. Then add the eggs one at a time. Stir the mixture to blend well.

Heat the olive oil in a large saucepan over low heat, bringing it to a temperature of about 110°F. It is helpful to use a thermometer to verify this temperature.

Pour the ^{1}/$_4$ cup of vegetable oil into a small bowl. You will use

~ Saffron Pudding

this oil to grease your fingers so they do not stick to the dough. To form the pastries, prepare a 22-inch piping bag with a large-tip star nozzle and fill it with the flour and semolina mixture. Squeeze the bag until 1^1/$_2$ to 2 inches of dough come out of the tip; with your other (oiled) hand, break off the dough and drop it into the hot olive oil. Do not put too many pastries in the oil at one time. Raise the heat to medium. Cook the pastries about 20 minutes, or until they are golden brown. Remove them from the saucepan with a slotted spoon to drain off the excess oil, then place them in the cold syrup for 30 minutes to absorb it.

Remove the pastries from the syrup with a slotted spoon to drain off some of the excess syrup, and serve them cold.

~~~~~~~~~~~~~~~~~~~~~

Zerde

Saffron Pudding

SERVES 6

This pudding is traditionally served at weddings and on holidays. It gets its rich yellow color from saffron.

^{1}/$_2$ teaspoon saffron

1 tablespoon currants

^{1}/$_3$ cup short-grain rice

1 cup sugar

^{1}/$_3$ cup rose water

3 tablespoons arrowroot or cornstarch

1 tablespoon pine nuts

1 tablespoon pomegranate seeds

1 tablespoon shelled and ground pistachios

Soak the saffron in ^{1}/$_4$ cup hot water for about 20 minutes. At the same time, soak the currants in warm water for about 15 minutes. Drain them and set them aside.

Meanwhile, place the rice and 4^1/$_2$ cups water in a medium-size saucepan and bring it to a boil. Simmer the mixture for about 25 minutes. Add the soaked saffron and its water along with the sugar, rose water, and arrowroot. Stir them well and simmer for about 4 minutes, until the pudding is thickened. Pour the pudding into individual serving cups and top with the currants, pine nuts, pomegranate seeds, and pistachios. Let the pudding cool at room temperature, then chill it for at least 30 minutes. Serve cold.

~~~~~~~~~~~~~~~~

Süzme Yoğurt Tatlısı

Yogurt Cake

MAKES 12 SERVINGS

SYRUP

   2½ cups cold water

   3 cups sugar

   2 tablespoons lemon juice

   8 eggs, room temperature, separated

   ½ cup sugar

   2 teaspoons lemon zest

   1 cup fine-grain semolina

   ¾ cup unbleached all-purpose flour, sifted, plus extra
      for dusting

   3 teaspoons baking powder

   2 cups Süzme Yogurt (page 11) at room temperature

   Pinch of salt

   ¼ cup finely ground pistachio nuts

   Thick Turkish Cream (page 146), whipped cream, or
      fresh berries, to serve

Preheat the oven to 350°F.

To make the syrup, combine the water and sugar and boil for 3 minutes. Lower the heat and simmer, uncovered, for about 15 minutes. Stir in the lemon juice and let the syrup cool.

Lightly butter and flour the inside of a 10 x 15 x 2-inch baking pan. Keep the pan in the refrigerator until you're ready to use it.

In a large mixing bowl, beat the egg yolks with the sugar and lemon zest until the mixture becomes slightly foamy. Gently fold in the semolina, flour, and baking powder. Then fold in the süzme yogurt. Stir the mixture until it's well blended.

Using an electric mixer or a wire whisk, beat the egg whites with a pinch of salt until they form firm peaks, about 3 to 4 minutes. Gently fold the egg whites into the semolina and flour mixture. Pour the batter into the prepared baking pan and spread it out evenly. Bake it on the center rack of the oven for about 45 minutes, or until it's a light golden brown.

Remove the pan from the oven and cut the cake into 12 squares. Pour the cooled syrup over the squares and let them sit at room temperature until they're cool. Before serving, sprinkle on the pistachio nuts. Serve with thick Turkish cream (page 146), whipped cream, or berries.

~~~~~~~~~~~~~~~~

Peynir Tatlısı

Feta Cheese Cakes

MAKES 6

This cake is made with white cheese (feta cheese) that is soaked overnight in hot water to remove the salt. It is a specialty of İzmir, and a famous dessert shop there called Riza Aksüt is famous for it.

   1⅓ cup good quality feta cheese

   2 tablespoons sugar

   6 tablespoons unsalted clarified butter (page 7)

   1½ tablespoons plus 1 teaspoon baking powder

   3 tablespoons heavy cream

   3 eggs at room temperature

   1 cup whole wheat flour, sifted

   4 tablespoons cornstarch

   Thick Turkish Cream (page 146), to serve

SYRUP

   3 cups cold water

   2 cups sugar

   1 tablespoon lemon juice

Cut the cheese into 1-inch cubes and soak them in a bowl of hot tap water for about 2 hours, changing the water frequently. Refrigerate the soaking cheese overnight so all of the salt leaches out.

The next day, preheat the oven to 375°F and grease the bottom of a heavy-bottomed 14 x 18 x 1-inch baking pan with a little butter.

Drain the cheese and squeeze out the excess water. Break it into small pieces by pushing it through a fine strainer into a bowl.

In another bowl, mix the sugar, butter, and baking powder. Add the cheese and the cream and mix well with a wooden spoon. Add the eggs one at a time and blend them well. Then add the flour and cornstarch and mix for about 1 minute, until all the ingredients are well incorporated. Do not overmix.

Fill a 22-inch piping bag that has a large-tip star nozzle with the mixture and pipe it onto the greased baking pan, making 6 cakes, each 4 inches in diameter. Bake them for about 25 minutes, or until the tops are lightly colored.

In the meantime, make the syrup by combining the cold water with the sugar and bringing it to a boil. Boil it for 5 minutes, then lower the heat and simmer the syrup, uncovered, for about 15

~~~~~~~~~~~~~~~~~

Ayran

Yogurt Drink

SERVES 6

This refreshing drink is popular all over Turkey, especially in the summer. In some villages it is made in large wooden barrels and is churned to make it frothy. Ayran often accompanies kebabs, koftas, and other meat dishes as well as böreks and pilafs.

> 1 quart plain yogurt
> 1 cup crushed ice
> 1 1/2 cups cold water
> Salt

Place the yogurt in a bowl with the crushed ice and the cold water. Season with salt to taste. Whisk the yogurt until it's frothy and serve it at once. Alternatively, whisk all the ingredients in a blender or food processor.

~~~~~~~~~~~~~~~~~

Vişne Şerbeti

Sour Cherry Drink

SERVES 6

Fruit juices are very popular in Turkey. Years ago, in the big cities, there were many small shops where fresh juices were sold. Now there are only a few such shops, and juices are purchased bottled or canned.

> 2 cups sugar
> 1 1/2 pounds fresh sour cherries
> 5 cups water

Combine the sugar with the water in a medium-size saucepan and stir the mixture over low heat until the sugar has dissolved. Add the cherries and simmer for about 20 minutes. Using a slotted spoon, remove the cherries from the pan. Pass them through a strainer, pressing them to extract all the juice. Discard the cherries. Chill the juice for at least 30 minutes and serve over crushed ice.

~~~~~~~~~~~~~~~~~

Gül Suyu Şerbeti

Rose Water Drink

SERVES 6

This drink is prepared mostly in small towns and villages for special occasions.

> 1 1/2 pounds rose petals, red or pink, scented and
>   pesticide-free
> 5 cups water
> 2 cups sugar
> 2 tablespoons lemon juice
> 1 tablespoon pine nuts

Wash the rose petals under running cold water and place them in a medium-size, nonreactive saucepan with the water. Add the sugar and the lemon juice. Bring the mixture to a boil, then simmer for about 20 minutes. Cover the saucepan and chill 4 to 6 hours.

In a small saucepan over high heat, stir the pine nuts for about 1 minute until they're golden.

Strain the rose-petal liquid through a double thickness of cheesecloth. Divide it among 6 cups and top each serving with the pan-roasted pine nuts.

VARIATION: Instead of rose petals and 5 cups of water, you can use 1 cup of bottled pure rose water and 4 cups of water.

~*Above:* Rose Water Drink
~*Overleaf:* Turkish coffee (page 150) with Turkish Delight (recipe not included) and Baklava (page 137)

RESOURCES

~ ~ ~ ~ ~ ~ ~ ~ ~ ~ ~ ~ ~ ~ ~ ~ ~

Ari's Deli and Market

10515 McFadden #101-104

Garden Grove, CA 96843

Tel: (714) 531-2747

Fax: (714) 531-0253

Dean and Deluca

560 Broadway

New York, NY 10012

Tel: (800) 221-7714

**Ethnic International
  Holding, Inc.**

PO Box 514

Cranbury, NJ 08512

Tel: (609) 395-8513

Fax: (609) 395-8603

Kalustyan's

123 Lexington Avenue

New York, NY 10016

Tel: (212) 685-3451

Fax: (212) 683-8458

International Food Bazaar

915 SW 9th

Portland, OR 97205

Tel: (503) 228-1960

Fax: (503) 228-1999

Kayseri Basterma Inc.

4 Vassar Road

Poughkeepsie, NY 12603

Tel: (888) KAYSERI or 529-7374

Tel: (914) 462-1710

Fax: (914) 462-2501

**Shallah's Middle Eastern
  Importing Co.**

290 White Street

Danbury, CT 06810

Tel: (203) 743-4181

Sahara Mart

106 East 2nd Street

Bloomington, IN 47401

Tel: (812) 333-0502

**Turquoise Cafe and Gourmet
  Market**

153 Sutherland Road

Brighton, MA 02135

Tel: (617) 277-5400

Fax: (617) 522-9176

For an updated list of sources for ingredients, call Periplus Editions toll free in the United States at (800) 526-2778.

ACKNOWLEDGMENTS

~ ~ ~ ~ ~ ~ ~ ~ ~ ~ ~ ~ ~ ~ ~ ~ ~

Special heartfelt thanks go to my editor, Isabelle Bleecker, and to the entire staff at Periplus Editions; thanks to Carl Tremblay, an astonishing photographer and his fine crew, Jill Winitzer for her beautiful book design, and George Simons for his special touch with food. A warm thank you to Nancy Anthony, who helped me through all the stages of the book and, finally, thanks to my fine kitchen staff.

~ ~

The publisher would like to thank the many people and shops for items that appear in the photographs: Alianza Contemporary Crafts, Boston, and artist Eileen Jager; Bean's gallery, Brookline, Massachusetts, and artist Kay Young; Country Floors, Inc. for ceramic tiles; Crate & Barrel; artist Alev Danis for her handcrafted plates from Shake the Tree Gallery, Brookline, Massachusetts, and her beautiful mosaics; The Denby Pottery Company of Freeport, Maine; Kitchen Arts, Boston; Maxwell's Pottery Outlet, of Freeport, Maine; Mohr & McPherson, Cambridge, Massachusetts; Newbury Imports, Boston; Pottery Barn; La Ruche, Boston; The Society of Arts and Crafts, Boston, and artists Karen Futral and Joe Spoon; Stone's Throw Gallery, Brookline, Massachusetts, and artists Janet Albert and Lynn Latimer; and especially Mari Quirk of Associated Quirks, for her beautiful backgrounds and surfaces.

~ ~

The publisher would also like to thank the following people for their gracious assistance in the preparation of this book: Madeleine Bleecker, Maggie Carr, Andrea Chesman, Lea Cohen, Jill Feron, Kim Frazee, Beth Ann Gerstein, Jessica Gallagher at Crate & Barrel, Kim Grogan, Paula Kesseli, Katie King, Marion Klausner, Steve Lamont, Janet McHugh, Deane Norton, Cecil and Arline Ross, Kathryn Sky-Peck, Edana Spicker, David VanLuven, Pat VanWagoner, Roberta and Al Winitzer.

INDEX

~~~~~~

Recipe names in *italic* indicate vegetarian recipes or recipes with vegetarian options. Note: all desserts and drinks are vegetarian as well. Page numbers in **boldface** indicate photographs.